TEXAS NOTARY PUBLIC GUIDE

By Jason Koneman

DISCLAIMER

I am not an attorney licensed to practice law and nothing in this book should be construed as legal advice or as a substitute for legal advice. This book is intended as a practical guide to augment and aid your own research and not as a legal manual. Current law should be followed at all times and takes precedent over this or any other notary manual or guide.

First Edition

ISBN: 1499386524
ISBN-13: 978-1499386523

Table of Contents

Foreword

Using a notary public to witness a signature is an important tool for risk management, which is useful in a wide variety of situations. When notarizing a document, the notary public is essentially certifying (1) the identity of the witness, and (2) the fact that the witness is signing the document willingly, both of which could be grounds for denying the authenticity of a document in the absence of proper notarization.

This process adds an additional layer of veracity to the document and serves as a deterrent to fraud. The importance of notarization applies in both informal and formal transactions, including contracts, deeds, powers of attorney, and wills. It is especially important in the context of litigation, where the truthfulness of a witness can impact the entire case. In the case of litigation, it is essential that any written sworn statements, or affidavits, are notarized in order to support the argument for their admissibility.

In the event that a document is notarized incorrectly, the risk management benefits of notarization may not apply. A simple error on the part of a notary has the potential to impact the outcome of a transaction or a matter in litigation. For that reason, it is imperative that the notary public be familiar with and follow the laws governing their role as outlined herein.

By:

Rachel N. Collins, JD
Attorney at Law

Chapter 1

Introduction

About Texas Notaries Public

A Notary Public is an Officer of the State of Texas who serves as a disinterested third party and is responsible for authenticating that the person who is signing a document is who they say they are within the document, that they are signing the document willingly and that they understand what the document is for and what the document accomplishes.

The Secretary of State of Texas website clearly explains what a Notary Public is and what their function is:

> *A Notary Public is a public servant with statewide jurisdiction who is authorized to take acknowledgments, protest instruments permitted by law to be protested (primarily negotiable instruments and bills and notes), administer oaths, take depositions, and certify copies of documents not recordable in the public records.*

> *A Notary Public is, in the true sense of the word, "a public servant" and "an officer of the State of Texas", conveniently located in the community so that the notary may be of service to the public. Each Notary Public takes an official oath of office to faithfully*

> *perform the duties of the office, and to insure such performance, a notary public is required to post a $10,000.00 bond with the Secretary of State. (Texas Secretary of State, 2014)*

Notaries public acknowledge that a document was signed by the person whose name is indicated, they administer oaths or affirmations such as those on affidavits, they take depositions for use in court cases and they certify copies of certain types of documents. Notaries are vital to the fight against fraud and in maintaining confidence in business, legal and personal transactions.

A notary is considered a ministerial officer of the state; meaning that a Notary Public is a State Official who simply follows the law and does not create or issue rulings on the law. For example in a court room the clerk might be considered ministerial while the judge is a Judicial Officer who interprets and rules on the application of the law.

There is a misconception that having a document notarized makes that document "legal". It does not. Notarizing a document guarantees the identity of the signer(s) of the document; not the contents of the document it's self.

Becoming a Notary Public

Notaries in the State of Texas are appointed by the Secretary of State of Texas to serve a 4 year term and must be bonded. A notary may apply to renew their commission just prior to the expiration of their previous commission. There residency, age and criminal history requirements to become a notary public in the State of Texas. The next chapter discusses, in further detail, how to become a notary in the State of Texas.

Records and Responsibility

Integrity, impeccable record keeping and strict adherence to the law is vital for any notary public. You may very well be called to testify in court in relation to any document that you notarize. For example: If you notarize the signatures on a contract and one of the document signers later claims in court that the signature on the document is forged you are very likely to be called to testify to validate the signature. The accuracy and truthfulness of your testimony and records must be unquestionable.

You have a duty to the public verify the identities of the person(s) signing documents in your presence and to ensure that proper procedure is followed. The public depends upon this process when accepting a document that has been notarized.

Fees

Notaries public are paid on a fee basis for their work and the fees that may be charged are established by law. Under no circumstances are you to charge an amount higher than those allowed by law to be charged.

While notary fees are fairly minimal; you are allowed and in some cases required to charge other fees which can be quite profitable. For example you can charge travel expenses, waiting fees and fees for other services that you provide.

In summary a Notary Public is an officer of the state who helps ensure the integrity of business, legal and personal transactions and in doing so provides an invaluable service to their communities. Notaries are required to keep accurate and complete records and are compensated on a fee basis.

Chapter 2

Becoming a Texas Notary Public

Notaries public in the State of Texas are appointed and commissioned by the Secretary of State of Texas, after approval of an application, to serve four year terms.

Please note: These requirements are subject to legislative change and are accurate as of the date of publication of this book.

Requirements

The requirements to be commissioned as a notary are established section 406 of the Texas Government code.

To be eligible to be appointed and commissioned as a notary public each applicant shall:

- Be at least 18 years of age
- Be a resident of the State of Texas
- Not have a final conviction of a felony or a crime of moral turpitude

Each notary public must provide a bond payable to the Governor of the State of Texas in the amount of $10,000.00

How to apply

You can apply to become a notary public on the Texas Secretary of State's website at http://www.sos.state.tx.us/statdoc/notary-public.shtml or through a notary organization such as the American Association of Notaries or the National Notary Association.

If you apply directly with the Secretary of State of Texas you must also apply for a bond from a bonding company and have that company complete a section of your application.

When applying through an organization, such as the American Association of Notaries, they will usually take care of this for you as part of the notary "package" that they offer. I only have personal experience with the American Association of Notaries but other organizations, such as the National Notary Association, offer similar packages.

I bought their package for $79.99 + shipping (about $6) and it included:

- 4 year, $10,000.00 notary bond
- State filing fee
- Notary stamp
- Notary record book
- Notary public manual
- One year membership

The package was supposed to include a notary fee and display sign but I did not receive one. Together the notary bond and state filing fee are worth over $70.00, so I thought this package was a really good deal.

Rejection of Appointment

The Secretary of State, pursuant to the Texas Government Code, may reject or deny your application for appointment for "good cause".

Good cause includes:

- Final conviction for a crime of moral turpitude
- A false statement knowingly made in an application
- Failure to comply with Section 406.017 of the Texas Government Code (Practicing Law without a License and

Improper Advertising) [This section is discussed in detail in the "Prohibited Acts" chapter]

- Final conviction for violation of a law regulating notaries in Texas or any other state
- The imposition on the notary of any judgment or fine for violation of a law or rule regulating notaries
- Performing any notarization without the person whose signature is being notarized being personally present

Section 406 of the Texas Government Code also provides that if the Secretary of State's office does reject your application you are entitled to notice a hearing and have the right to appeal.

Section 406.009 of the Texas Government Code (b) states "An action by the Secretary of State under this section is subject to the rights of notice, hearing, adjudication and appeal."

Crimes of Moral Turpitude

A crime of moral turpitude is a crime that by its very nature is deemed to be wicked, dishonest or unjust.

According to an opinion issued by the Texas Attorney General (Opinion GA-0299) crimes of moral turpitude have historically been defined as

> *"Shameful wickedness - so extreme a departure from ordinary standards of honest[y], good morals, justice, or ethics as to be shocking to the moral sense of the community. It has also been defined as an act of baseness, vileness, or depravity in the private and social duties which one person owes to another, or to society in general, contrary to the accepted and customary rule of right and duty between people." (Attorney General of Texas, 2005)*

In the same opinion the Attorney General goes on to give a more modern definition of crime of moral turpitude as "dishonesty, fraud, deceit, misrepresentation, or deliberate violence".

So for instance accidentally writing a bad check may not be considered a crime or moral turpitude a crime such as check fraud or forging someone else's check most likely will be considered a crime of moral turpitude.

If you have a criminal conviction that you believe might disqualify you from being appointed as a notary public you can call and ask the Secretary of State's office or consult with a licensed attorney.

False Statement Made in an Application

This is a fairly straight-forward reason for disqualification. If you make an intentionally false statement in your application for appointment as a notary public your application will be denied.

For instance: if you state that you have never been convicted of a crime even though several years ago you were convicted of any offense, such as DWI or assault, then your application will be denied because you have made a false statement on your application.

Another example of a false statement would be an Oklahoma resident who uses the mailing address of a relative in Texas so that they may qualify for appointment then you have made a false statement on your application and it may be rejected or if approved your commission may later be revoked.

NEVER make a false statement on your application or in any other circumstance related to the office of notary public. Not only may you be denied appointment or have your commission revoked you may very well also be charged with fraud or perjury.

Failure to Comply with Section 406.017 of the Government Code

You may never give legal advice, accept fees for legal advice, represent yourself as an attorney or advertise yourself as a "notario publico".

This topic will be discussed in further detail in the "Prohibited Acts" chapter.

Final Conviction of Violating a Notary Law

If you have ever been finally convicted of violating a law pertaining to notaries public in any state within the United States you are not eligible for appointment as a notary public in Texas.

Likewise, if you are a notary in Texas and are convicted of a crime related to the office of notary public then your commission will be revoked.

This may be a crime such as notarizing a document without the signer being present or accepting an expired identification card from a person who is not personally known to you (in Texas you may notarize for a person who is personally known to you without requiring photo identification).

Crimes under this section may also include letting someone use your notary stamp, accepting a bribe, charging a fee greater than what is allowed or putting any date on a notary certificate other than the date on which you actually notarized the document.

Imposition of Penalties, Fines or Judgments Relating to the Duties of a Notary Public

If you have ever been fined or faced any other criminal or civil liability for violating notary laws then your application may be rejected or your commission revoked.

This goes further than the Final Conviction disqualifier in that even if you are never charged with a crime your application can be denied or your commission revoked if you are sued in civil court for something that was done in your official capacity as a notary public.

An example of this might be that you notarized a form to authorize the international travel of a minor but forgot to affix your notary stamp or seal. If your failure to affix a stamp or seal causes the child to miss the trip or causes a delay or cancellation of the vacation, with or without refund, you may be subject to a civil suit.

If the plaintiff in the suit is successful and receives a judgment against you then you may very well face disciplinary action, revocation of your commission or have a future application rejected.

Notarizing for a Person Not Personally Present

You absolutely must never notarize a document for a person who is not personally present before you. One of the most important rules, if not THE most important, for notaries is that the person whose signature you are notarizing must personally appear before you.

A person may not give permission or authorization for another person to notarize a document that has their name and signature on it. Even in the case of a Power of Attorney or Attorney-in-Fact you cannot notarize any person's signature without them being present. In this particular circumstance the attorney-in-fact will sign the document themselves as attorney-in-fact.

As I will discuss in another chapter on proper procedures, there is a verbal ceremony that must accompany every notarization or the notarization is invalid. How can you ask someone a question or place them under oath when they sign a document if they are not there with you? You can't.

Not only must a verbal ceremony take place but each time you notarize a document you are certifying on a legal document that someone has appeared before you. If you sign a certification that someone was before you when they were not you have just committed perjury.

Approval of Application

Once the Secretary of State approves your application for appointment as a notary public you will receive an email containing your commission certificate and some educational documents

Oath of Office

As a notary public is an officer of the state and as such the notary must take an oath of office before they can officially and legally execute the duties of notary public.

To execute your oath of office you can print and take your notary commission certificate (this will be in your approval email from the Secretary of State) to any notary public in the state. That notary will then administer your oath and affix his or her seal. After taking the oath you are officially a notary public for the State of Texas!

Seal and Journal

Before you can perform any notary duties you must purchase a seal or stamp and a journal. If you used an organization such as the American Association of Notaries and purchased one of their packages you will probably receive these items as part of that package.

I recommend purchasing a durable journal. Your journal will be opened and closed a lot and will face considerable wear and tear. You will be required to keep this journal for the entire length of your commission and maybe longer.

Another thing to consider when looking at notary journals is the page layout. Some journals have single entries that span across two pages whiles others have entries on single pages that may fit 5 total entries per page.

I recommend a journal that has the entire entry on one page. This makes it much easier to photocopy a journal entry if you ever need to provide a copy or certified copy to someone. Providing copies of your journal pages, upon request, is required by law.

Chapter 3

Duties and Authorities of a Notary Public

Notaries in Texas have several very specific duties and legal authorities. Notaries can take acknowledgments or proofs of written documents, protest instruments permitted by law to be protested, administer oaths or affirmations, take depositions, certify copies of non-recordable documents, oversee the opening of safe deposit boxes and issue subpoenas in specific circumstances.

A notary may only perform acts in an official capacity that are specifically authorized by law and must never misrepresent their authorities or legal abilities.

Acknowledgments and Proofs of Written Instruments

An acknowledgment of a written instrument is one of the two main types of notarizations that an average notary public will do.

An acknowledgement is where a person comes before a notary and acknowledges that (s)he signed the document and that they signed willingly for the purposes stated therein.

A proof of a document is a statement by a witness to a document affirming that (s)he witnessed the execution of the document.

Unlike a jurat; a document requiring an acknowledgement may be signed before it is brought to the notary.

Proof by Handwriting

NOTE: Proof by handwriting should be done carefully as there are criteria that must be met. Please refer to the Applicable Laws chapter to read these requirements in detail.

Protests

Protests are very rarely done in the modern world with the adoption of the Universal Commercial Code. If you are unfamiliar with the laws regarding protests and which items may be protested then you should refrain from protesting instruments. It is acceptable to refuse to notarize a protest if you are unfamiliar with applicable laws.

A protest is a method by which a notary notifies a party that a financial instrument that has been presented for payment by the recipient has been returned unpaid.

Administration of Oaths and Affirmations

A notary public is authorized by law to administer oaths and affirmations. The notary certificate associated with and oath/affirmation is called a jurat.

An oath requires the person who is making the oath to swear to a god, deity or higher being that the statement being made or the information provided is true and accurate.

An affirmation has the same legal standing as an oath but does not invoke the name of a deity or higher power but still makes them certify that their statement and any information provided is true.

For example, in the verbal ceremony for an oath you might ask “Do you swear under penalties of perjury that the information contained in this document is the truth, so help you God?” In an affirmation you may ask “Do you affirm under penalties of perjury that the information contained in this document is the truth?”

When administering an oath or affirmation to someone I ask them to raise their right hand to signify to them that they are under oath. This way they know that any false statements made at this time are considered perjury.

Making a false statement to a notary in connection with his/her official duties is considered perjury and is a prosecutable offense.

Copy Certification

Copy certification is a process where a notary copies a document and certifies that the copy is a true and complete copy of the original document. The document being copy certified must NOT be a recordable document. Documents such as birth, death and marriage certificates are considered recordable documents and may not be copy certified by a notary public. A notary may not issue a copy certification for school transcripts unless they are certifying copies for the institution providing the transcripts. A notary may, however, copy certify a diploma.

There are several requirements for copy certification:

- A copy to be certified must come from the original document only. You cannot copy certify a copy of a copy.
- The copy must be made in black ink only, even on color documents.
- The notary must personally make the copy or completely and immediately supervise the entire copying process. So if someone else is operating the copying machine you must be standing beside them and witness the entire process.
- The document must not be a recordable document or an identification card of any type. There are instances where someone may need a copy of an identification card or passport for a visa or other travel document. The procedure for this will be discussed in the procedures chapter.

Copy certifications are done under such strict rules because of the nature of the act you are performing. By certifying a copy you are saying it is an exact copy of the original document. If you do not make the copy yourself or immediately supervise the copying then how do you know it is an exact copy?

Consider this: a person brings a sales contract to you that is several pages long and brings you what they claim is a photocopy of the same and asks you certify the copy. Now let's say that you comply with their request and provide the certificate. How do you know that the sales price for the item or service wasn't altered from $2,500.00 to $25,000.00?

By notarizing this copy certification you could potentially open yourself up to a $22,500.00 liability, plus court costs. Liability will be discussed in further detail in the liability chapter.

Taking of Depositions

Another duty of a notary is take depositions used in legal proceedings. When you take a deposition you place the person being deposed under oath so that they know the information provided must be truthful.

The notary collects and verifies the information provided and issues a certification stating that the answers included are those of the person being deposed.

Subpoenas

Black's Law Dictionary defines a subpoena as a "the usual writ for the summoning of witnesses or the submission of evidence, as records or documents, before a court or other deliberative body." (Dictionary.com, 2014)

A subpoena is an extremely serious legal document and should only be issued when absolutely necessary and every effort must be taken to ensure it has been issued appropriately and in full accordance with the law.

A subpoena issued by a notary public generally has the same weight as if it were issued by a District Judge.

A notary public who fails to follow proper procedure in relation to the issuance of a subpoena may be subject to disciplinary action by the Texas Secretary of State.

Section 406 of the Texas Government Code does not specifically authorize a notary to issue subpoenas; but this authority is granted in other sections of law and code.

Failure of a recipient of a subpoena to comply with subpoena may subject them to Contempt of Court or other civil and criminal penalties which may include fines, jail time or both.

Depositions

Rule 176.4 of the Texas Rules of Civil Procedure specifically authorizes any officer who is authorized to take depositions, such as a notary public, to issue a subpoena to compel testimony at a deposition.

The rule says that upon request and presentation of a notice of deposition the officer shall immediately issue a subpoena that will be served with the notice of deposition.

Proofs of Documents

Section 121.013(a) of the Texas Civil Practice and Remedies Code specifically allows an officer authorized to take proofs of instruments to issue a subpoena to compel a witness or signer of a document to testify about the execution of the document.

> *On the sworn application of a person interested in the proof of an instrument required or permitted by law to be recorded, stating that a witness to the instrument refuses to appear and testify regarding the execution of the instrument and that the instrument cannot be*

> *proven without the evidence of the witness, an officer authorized to take proofs of instruments shall issue a subpoena requiring the witness to appear before the officer and testify about the execution of the instrument.*

In summary a notary public in the state of Texas has the limited authority to issue a subpoena and should only do so in accordance with the strict requirements of the law. Subpoenas will generally be issued while working with or for an attorney, but may be issued on behalf of a person representing themselves in court.

Chapter 4

Prohibited Acts

There are several things that Texas notaries are specifically and absolutely prohibited from doing. The Texas Secretary of State has published a list of Prohibited Acts on their website (Texas Secretary of State, 2014). A notary shall not:

- Perform acts which constitute practice of law (unless you are an attorney licensed to practice law)
- Prepare, draft, select or give advice concerning legal documents
- Use the phrase "notario" or "notario publico" to advertise notary services
- Overcharge for notary public services
- Notarize a document without the signer being in the notary's presence
- Notarize the notary's own signature
- Issue identification cards
- Sign a notarial certificate under any other names than the one under which the notary was commissioned
- Record in the notary's record book the identification number that was assigned by the governmental agency or by the United States to the signer, grantor or maker and that is set forth on an identification card or passport; or any other number that could be used to identify the signer, grantor or maker of the document. (This does not prohibit a notary from recording a number related to the residence or alleged residence of the signer, grantor or maker of the document or the instrument.

Unauthorized Practice of Law

Section 406.017 of the Texas Government Code specifically prohibits a notary public, who is not an attorney licensed to practice law, to represent themselves as an attorney or perform an act which constitutes the practice of law.

As a non-attorney notary you are not allowed to give any information that can be construed as legal advice or the practice of law. You cannot help the signer prepare or edit the document to be notarized (with the exception of making them fill-in or cross out blank spaces within the document).

Even printing a stock form from the internet for a client can be considered the practice of law. If you want to allow a client to use your computer to print a stock form from the internet you may do so, but you cannot help them search for or select the document. You cannot tell them which document to print.

You cannot explain to the signer what the document is for, how it works or provide instructions on how to complete the form.

If a client asks you for any of this information simply tell them that you are not an attorney and that you are prohibited from providing that information by law.

Selecting Notary Certificates

If a signer or client comes to you with a document to be notarized and the document does not contain a notary certificate you may allow them to select a stock certificate from your inventory, but you may not select a certificate to attach to the document.

You should give the signer several certificates to choose from such as a jurat, acknowledgement and verification and ask them to select one. If they are unable to select a notary certificate then you must refuse to notarize the document and invite them to return once they have selected one or once they have received advice from an attorney as to which certificate type to use.

While you cannot select a notary certificate for a signer or client you can make changes to the certificate so that it is true and correct. Notary certificates and samples of each can be found in the following chapter.

Notario and Notario Publico

You may never use the phrases "notario" or "notario publico" when advertising notary services. The literal translation of notary into Spanish is "notario"; however the function of a notario is closer to that of an attorney. Advertising yourself as a notario is akin to advertising yourself as an attorney.

If you ever place an ad in Spanish you must not translate the phrases notary or notary public. Additionally you must include the following statement in both English and Spanish:

> *"I AM NOT AN ATTORNEY LICENSED TO PRACTICE LAW IN TEXAS AND MAY NOT GIVE LEGAL ADVICE OR ACCEPT FEES FOR LEGAL ADVICE."*

That statement must be prominent in the advertisement and must be the same size or larger than the other text in the ad.

Advertising and marketing will be discussed in further detail in a following chapter.

Overcharging for Notary Services

The Texas Government Code lists the maximum fee that can be charged for a notary service. You are strictly prohibited from charging any more than the prescribed maximum.

Maximum Notary Fees in Texas are as follows:

Service	Fee
Protesting a bill or note for non-acceptance or non-payment, register and seal	$4.00
Each notice of protest	$1.00
Protesting in all other cases	$4.00
Certificate and seal to a protest	$4.00
Taking the acknowledgment or proof of any deed or other instrument in writing, for registration, including certificate and seal	
(1) for the first signature	$6.00
(2) for each additional signature	$1.00
Administering an oath or affirmation with certificate and seal	$6.00
All certificates under seal not otherwise provided for	$6.00
Copies of all records and papers in the notary Public's office, for each page	$0.50
Taking the depositions of witnesses, for each 100 words	$0.50
Swearing a witness to a deposition, certificate, seal and other business connected with taking the deposition	$6.00
All notarial acts not provided for	$6.00

Notary fees are not subject to sales tax.

Though these are the maximum fees you can charge for notary fees you are allowed to charge for other fees such as travel, waiting fees, etc... Texas law also specifically states that an officer of the state must bill the client for any expenses incurred.

Notarizing Your Own Signature

A notary public may not notarize his or her own signature on any document with the exception that a notary may sign a notary certificate for certified copies, depositions and certified copies of notarial records or any in any other manner directly required with the duties of notary public.

A notary must be impartial in all notarial acts and it is impossible to be impartial if you are notarizing your own signature. The premise behind have a document notarized is that an impartial and disinterested third party is confirming the identity of the signer and is verifying that the document was signed for the purposes stated therein.

You may issue a copy certification or certification of copies of your notarial records.

Signing a Notarial Certificate Under a Different Name

A notary may only sign a certificate under the name in which his/her commission is issued.

For instance if your full name is John Michael Doe and your commission is in the name "John M. Doe" then you may not sign a certificate as John Doe or John Michael Doe, only as John M. Doe.

In the case of a name change due to marriage or court order you can continue signing in your old name until you renew or you may apply for a name change on your notary commission. Contact the Secretary of State's office for more information.

Recording an Identification Number in Your Journal

Texas law requires that you verify the identity of signers of documents that you notarize but strictly prohibits you from recording the identification number.

A notary public's journal is a public record and must be made for inspection by the general public. Also, if requested, you must provide a copy of any page of your journal to any person making the request.

If you had identification numbers recorded along with copies of people's signatures, full names and addresses you would be a gold mine for forgers and identity thieves.

If you mistakenly or inadvertently record an identification number in your journal you should redact that information from any copies you provide.

You should also notify the recipient of the copy that this information has been redacted.

Chapter 5

Notarial Certificates

There are standard formats for notarial certificates established by law. You must use these notary certificates or use a certificate with substantially similar wording.

Correcting Mistakes

A notary is not only authorized, but is required, to correct a mistake in a notary certificate. For example if a certificate says that the notarization took place in Galveston County but actually took place in Harris County then you must correct the certificate to reflect the proper venue.

When making a correction on a notary certificate never use white-out or completely cover the item being corrected. Instead you simply mark a single line through the incorrect info and write the correct info above or beside it and initial.

Example:

State of Texas

Harris J.K

County of ~~Galveston~~

Venue

Every notary certificate must contain a venue. The venue indicates where the notarization of the document physical took place and is in the format of:

State of Texas

County of ____________________

Since a Texas notary public has jurisdiction statewide (s)he may notarize documents in any county within the borders of the state. A Texas notary may not notarize a document outside of the state of Texas even if it is for use within the state of Texas.

A notary certificate that does not contain a venue is invalid.

The following forms and form language are found in various sections of Texas law.

Acknowledgments

Chapter 121 of the Texas Civil Practice and Remedies Code lays out requirements for notary acknowledgment certificates.

Ordinary Certificate of Acknowledgment

Section 121.007: The form of an ordinary certificate of acknowledgment must be substantially as follows:

The State of ______________,
County of ______________,

Before me ______________ (here insert the name and character of the officer) on this day personally appeared __________________, known to me (or proved to me on the oath of __________________ or through ____________________ (description of identity card or other document)) to be the person whose name is subscribed to the foregoing instrument and acknowledged to me that he executed the same for the purposes and consideration therein expressed.

(Seal) Given under my hand and seal of office this _________ day of ___________, A.D., _________.

(seal) (Signature of Officer)

(Title of Officer)

Acknowledgment Short Forms

Section 121.008: (a) The forms for certificates of acknowledgment provided by this section may be used as alternatives to other authorized forms. They may be referred to as "statutory forms of acknowledgment."

(b) Short forms for certificates of acknowledgment include:

For a natural person acting in his own right

State of Texas

County of ____________

This instrument was acknowledged before me on (date) by (name or names of person or persons acknowledging).

(Signature of officer)

(Title of officer)

My commission expires: ________

For a natural person as principal acting by attorney-in-fact

State of Texas

County of ____________

This instrument was acknowledged before me on (date) by (name of attorney-in-fact) as attorney-in-fact on behalf of (name of principal).

(Signature of officer)

(Title of officer)

My commission expires: ________

For a partnership acting by one or more partners

State of Texas

County of ____________

This instrument was acknowledged before me on (date) by (name of acknowledging partner or partners), partner(s) on behalf of (name of partnership), a partnership.

(Signature of officer)

(Title of officer)

My commission expires: ________

For a corporation

State of Texas

County of ____________

This instrument was acknowledged before me on (date) by (name of officer), (title of officer) of (name of corporation acknowledging) a (state of incorporation) corporation, on behalf of said corporation.

(Signature of officer)

(Title of officer)

My commission expires: ________

For a public officer, trustee, executor, administrator, guardian, or other representative

State of Texas

County of ____________

This instrument was acknowledged before me on (date) by (name of representative) as (title of representative) of (name of entity or person represented).

(Signature of officer)

(Title of officer)

My commission expires: ________

Proof by Witness

Section 121.010 of the Civil Procedures and Remedies Code: When the execution of a written instrument is proved by a witness, the certificate of the officer must be substantially as follows:

The State of ____________,

County of ____________.

Before me, ________ (here insert the name and character of the officer), on this day personally appeared ____________, known to me (or proved to me on the oath of ____________), to be the person whose name is subscribed as a witness to the foregoing instrument of writing, and after being duly sworn by me stated on oath that he saw ____________, the grantor or person who executed the foregoing instrument, subscribe the same (or that the grantor or person who executed such instrument of writing acknowledged in his presence that he had executed the same for the purposes and consideration therein expressed), and that he had signed the same as a witness at the request of the grantor (or person who executed the same.)

(Seal) Given under my hand and seal of office this ______ day of ____________, A.D., ____________."

Execution of a Will

Texas Probate Code Section 59 governs the execution of wills. The language provided for the notary certificate is as follows:

THE STATE OF TEXAS
COUNTY OF ________________

Before me, the undersigned authority, on this day personally appeared _______________, _______________, and _______________, known to me to be the testator and the witnesses, respectively, whose names are subscribed to the annexed or foregoing instrument in their respective capacities, and, all of said persons being by me duly sworn, the said _______________, testator, declared to me and to the said witnesses in my presence that said instrument is his last will and testament, and that he had willingly made and executed it as his free act and deed; and the said witnesses, each on his oath stated to me, in the presence and hearing of the said testator, that the said testator had declared to them that said instrument is his last will and testament, and that he executed same as such and wanted each of them to sign it as a witness; and upon their oaths each witness stated further that they did sign the same as witnesses in the presence of the said testator and at his request; that he was at that time eighteen years of age or over (or being under such age, was or had been lawfully married, or was then a member of the armed forces of the United States or of an auxiliary thereof or of the Maritime Service) and was of sound mind; and that each of said witnesses was then at least fourteen years of age.

____
Testator

____
Witness

____
Witness

Subscribed and sworn to before me by the said ____________, testator, and by the said _________________ and ________________, witnesses, this ______ day of _________________ A.D. _________________.

(SEAL) ______________________

(Signature)

Copies of the sample certificates that are provided by the Texas Secretary of State in the educational materials packet sent with your notary commission can be found at the following web address: http://www.sos.state.tx.us/statdoc/forms/edinfo-sample-forms.pdf.

Chapter 6

Records, Allowable Fees and Other Requirements

To properly and legally perform notarization within the state of Texas you must keep proper records, certify notarizations with your seal of office and you must abide by the maximum fee schedules as permitted by law.

Records

You must keep proper notarial records including a notary ledger or journal. Remember: anything written in your journal or kept in your notarial records is public information and is subject to disclosure or inspection upon request by any person.

Specifically Section 406.014 of the Texas Government Code requires the following elements of each notarization to be recorded in a journal:

- the date of each instrument notarized
- the date of the notarization
- the name of the signer, grantor or maker
- the signer's, grantor's or maker's residence or alleged residence
- whether the signer, grantor or maker is personally known by the notary public, was identified by an identification or a passport issued by the United States, or was introduced to the notary public
    - If introduced, the name and residence or alleged residence of the individual introducing the signer, grantor or maker.

- If the instrument is proved by a witness, the residence of the witness, whether the witness is personally known by the notary public or was introduced to the notary public
    - if introduced, the name and residence of the individual introducing the witness
- The name and residence of the grantee
- If land is conveyed or charged by the instrument, the name of the original grantee and the county where the land is located
- A brief description of the instrument.

A notary public is also required to keep in his or her notarial records a copy of each document that has been copy certified. If a client asks you to copy certify a document in accordance with the copy certification requirements you are to make an extra copy and keep it in your official notarial records.

If you refuse notary services to an individual you should make a journal entry describing the document and the circumstances that led to your refusal.

If anything odd or out of the ordinary occurs during the notarization it should be listed in the note section. This helps completely document the notarization and may help you remember the notarization if you ever asked about it in the future.

Also be sure and indicate in the notes if the client has chosen one of your stock certificates. This will help document that you did not choose the form for the client.

Inspection and Copies of Records

All notary public records in the state of Texas are considered public information must be made accessible to the general public upon request.

Section 406.014(b) of the Texas Government Code plainly states "Entries in the notary's book are public information."

Section 406.014(c) also states "A notary public shall, on payment of all fees, provide a certified copy of any record in the notary public's office to any person requesting the copy."

It is considered a violation of notary law to refuse access to your journal or other notarial records to any person requesting them.

While any person has the right to review the documents and your journal they may never leave your possession. You should be in the same room as the person looking at your records at all times. It is a crime for any person other than the notary to possess the notary's record book or journal.

Tampering With Notary Records

You must never allow any person to make any alterations, changes or marks in or to your notary records. It is a crime under Chapter 37.10 of the Texas Penal Code for any person to tamper with a governmental record.

False Entries

Never make a false entry in your journal or in any other official notary record. It is a criminal offense to do so and may result in fines, prison time or both.

This not only includes adding records for notarizations that never took place but includes back dating (or future dating) a journal entry, recording an incorrect fee amount or any other false information added to the record.

Miscellaneous Records

There are times when you might want to record some pertinent information, other than notary entries, in your record book.

For instance if you are unsure how to handle a particular notarization request you can call the Secretary of State's office and ask for guidance. Whatever advice they give you, write it in your journal at the next available open entry and date it. This way you have chronological entry with details on how that situation should be handled.

Also, if your notary stamp is ever lost, stolen or damaged you should make an entry in the book with the date of loss. Another good idea is to change ink colors of your stamp if this ever happens and note in your journal that your ink color has changed and include a sample impression of your new stamp. This way if someone uses your old stamp your journal will reflect when that stamp was no longer in your possession.

Fee Book

All notaries in Texas are required to keep a fee book to document fees collected. Most notary journals will have a place to list notary fees and this will satisfy the requirement for a fee book.

Disposition of Records After Leaving Office

After you leave the office of notary public you should deposit all journals and records in your possession with the County Clerk in the county of your residence at the time of you leaving office.

Fees

As we discussed earlier the state has established statutory maximums on the fees a notary may charge. In this section we will discuss three types of fees: Notary Fees, Non-Notary Fees and Expenses incurred by the notary on behalf of a client.

You must always be prepared to issue a receipt to any person who you charge any fees. Amazon.com has a pre-printed notary receipt book that is pretty nice. I keep one of these pads in my notary bag all the time.

Notary Fees

As shown earlier, the statutory maximum fees for notary services are as follows:

Service	Fee
Protesting a bill or note for non-acceptance or non-payment, register and seal	$4.00
Each notice of protest	$1.00
Protesting in all other cases	$4.00
Certificate and seal to a protest	$4.00
Taking the acknowledgment or proof of any deed or other instrument in writing, for registration, including certificate and seal	
(1) for the first signature	$6.00
(2) for each additional signature	$1.00
Administering an oath or affirmation with certificate and seal	$6.00
All certificates under seal not otherwise provided for	$6.00
Copies of all records and papers in the notary Public's office, for each page	$0.50
Taking the depositions of witnesses, for each 100 words	$0.50
Swearing a witness to a deposition, certificate, seal and other business connected with taking the deposition	$6.00
All notarial acts not provided for	$6.00

Example 1: A couple comes to you with an authorization of foreign travel with minor form that they need so their child can go on a church

trip. The notary certificate is for an acknowledgement and requires both parents to sign.

The maximum fee for the first signature on an acknowledgment is $6.00 and the maximum fee for each additional signature is $1.00. In this case you can only charge up to $7.00 for your services.

Example 2: A member of the public comes in and would like to inspect your notary journal. After looking through the journal they find an entry that they would like a copy of. This person asks you for a certified copy of that entry. The fee for a copy of one page in the notary's records is $0.50 and the fee for "all certificates under seal not otherwise provided for" is $6.00; so you may charge the client $6.50.

If you overcharge for notary services you will face disciplinary action from the Secretary of State which could include revocation of your commission and possibly criminal charges. Another penalty is that you will be forced to pay the person you overcharged up to four times the amount overcharged.

Non-Notary Fees

In addition to notary fees a notary can charge other fees such as for travel, waiting time, fax and photocopying services and any other miscellaneous charges.

Mobile notary services can be quite profitable. I have seen mobile notaries that charge a minimum of $50.00 for travel expenses; in addition to the fees they charge for the notary service.

Example: A client calls you from the airport and needs a document notarized right away but they cannot leave the airport to get to a notary. The document is a simple acknowledgement requiring one signature. When you get to the airport you can charge the client a travel fee of $40.00, for example, and $6.00 for the notarization.

It is very important that the travel fee be agreed upon in advance and that you get a signed and itemized receipt. This way there can never be a question of you overcharging for notary services.

Also bear in mind that notary fees are not subject to sales tax but other fees you might charge may be. For instance, copies and faxes are subject to sales tax. If you will be offering these services you must apply for a Sales and Use Tax Permit before charging for these services.

Expenses Incurred for a Client

There may be times when you incur an expense on behalf of a client. This may include parking, tolls or any other expense that you incur on behalf of any particular client. You are absolutely allowed to charge these fees to the client.

Other Requirements

Seal

All official acts of a notary public are authenticated with a seal of office. The seal can either be an embossment, stamp or and electronic reproduction meeting the size and design requirements of a stamp or embossment. All seals must be photographically reproducible.

Section 406.013 of the Texas Government Code reads:

a) A notary public shall provide a seal of office that clearly shows, when embossed, stamped, or printed on a document, the words "Notary Public, State of Texas" around a star of five points, the notary public's name, and the date the notary public's commission expires. The notary public shall authenticate all official acts with the seal of office.

b) The seal may be a circular form not more than two inches in diameter or a rectangular form not more than one inch in width and 2-1/2 inches in length. The seal must have a serrated or milled edge border.

c) The seal must be affixed by a seal press or stamp that embosses or prints a seal that legibly reproduces the required elements of the seal under photographic methods. An indelible ink pad must be used for affixing by a stamp the impression of a seal on an instrument to authenticate the notary public's official act.

d) Subsection (c) does not apply to an electronically transmitted authenticated document, except that an electronically transmitted authenticated document must legibly reproduce the required elements of the seal.

Seal Security

You must never let someone else use your seal or grant anyone else access to your seal. You must never let an employer or supervisor control your seal.

Any person other than yourself, including another notary or spouse, who uses your seal with or without your permission to notarize a document or for any other purpose may be in violation of section 37.11 of the Texas Penal Code which makes it a felony of the third degree to impersonate a public official.

If your seal is lost you should promptly order a new seal and notify the Secretary of State's office. If your seal is stolen you should contact the police, file a police report and submit the police report along with a letter describing the theft to the Secretary of State.

Seal Color

The Texas Secretary of State recommends that you use a seal with black ink. All of the commercial impression inkers, for use with an embossing seal, which I have come across have been black ink.

I personally prefer to use a blue stamp and a blue pen to sign my name. This helps determine the original copy of a document.

Advertising

You must be cautious when advertising that you do not imply or give any sort of impression that you are an attorney or that you have any authority greater than you really do. Doing so will expose you to civil and criminal liability.

Texas has very strict laws regarding advertising notary services in any language other than English. As we discussed earlier you may never allow the words "notary" or "notary public" to be translated in to Spanish.

In addition, any time you advertise in a language other than English you must include the following statement in a conspicuous size and location:

> ***I AM NOT AN ATTORNEY LICENSED TO PRACTICE LAW IN TEXAS AND MAY NOT GIVE LEGAL ADICE OR ACCEPT FEES FOR LEGAL ADVICE.***

This statement should be in both English and the language of the advertisement.

You must also publish a copy of the statutory fee maximums.

Another thing to avoid is advertising as an immigration specialist. A notary public in Texas is not an immigration attorney or immigration officer. Advertising as an immigration specialist implies that you have knowledge and skills applicable especially to immigration. Unless you are an attorney licensed to practice law then you cannot be an immigration specialist.

Just as I am not a physician; I cannot advertise myself as a cardiac specialist just because I know CPR.

Errors and Omissions Insurance

There is no legal or regulatory requirement that you have Errors and Omissions (E&O) Insurance; however, it is HIGHLY recommended that you do. As a notary public you are responsible for every act that you do.

While E&O insurance won't protect you for deliberate wrongful acts, it will protect you from mistakes that can open you up to liability. Forgetting to date, sign or stamp a document can nullify the notarization and make you liable for any financial consequences that result.

For instance, if you forget to sign a notary certificate on a sales contract and the sale falls through or the seller is not able to legally recover the cost of the item sold from the purchaser as a result of your omission then you may be held liable for the losses of the seller. Liability will be discussed in further detail in a further chapter devoted specifically to liability.

Ownership of Supplies

No matter who purchases or pays for your commission, log book or seal you remain the sole owner of these items. Nobody is allowed to take or keep them from you or restrict your access to these items.

Your seal and records belong to your office as notary public, meaning to they belong to you in your official capacity.

Texas Attorney General Opinion GA-0723 plainly states that even after termination of employment the commission and supplies of a notary public remain the property of that notary public.

> Because a commission is issued to an individual notary, the notary's private employer may not take possession of or transfer the notary's book and seal after the notary leaves employment. The secretary of state may adopt rules to specify the details of the disposition of a notary's book and seal. (Attorney General of Texas, 2009)

If you find yourself in a situation where an employer or former employer refuses to allow you to keep your notary supplies or records you should inform them that they may make a photocopy of the records but that you retain ownership. If necessary you should provide a copy of Texas Attorney General Opinion GA-0723.

If they still refuse to allow you to retain possession of the supplies and records you should contact the police, provide a copy of that opinion and ask for them to have the employer return the items for you. You should also ask for a police report and forward it to the Secretary of State of Texas.

Chapter 7

Refusal of Services

A notary is an officer of the state and a public official. As such; the notary has a duty to uphold the law and the constitutions of both the state and of the United States.

A notary has not only a right but a duty to refuse notary services in certain circumstances. However, a notary must not discriminate against any person or any group of persons.

Valid Refusals

Here are a few situations in which a notary may refuse services to any person. If you ever refuse notary services to someone you should make a journal entry describing the refusal and the reason behind it.

As will be discussed in the next chapter, Proper Procedures, the first thing I always do is start the journal entry and get the identification of the person for whom I am notarizing. If you record the person's information in the journal before you review the document then you will have the necessary information to either record a complete notarization or a refusal.

Chapter 87.30 of the Texas Administrative Code authorizes circumstances in which a notary may refuse notary services.

(a) A notary is authorized to refuse to perform a notarial act if:
   (1) the notary has reasonable grounds to believe that the signer is acting under coercion or undue influence

(2) the notary has reasonable grounds to believe that the document in connection with which the notarial act is requested may be used for an unlawful or improper purpose
(3) the notary has concerns about the capacity of the signing party to understand the contents of the document
(4) the notary is not familiar with the type of notarization requested

Also, an employer may limit the notary services of an employee who is a notary during work hours, but may not limit your services during non-work hours.

Fraud

One of the primary functions of the notary in society is to help prevent fraud. If you have any indication or perception of fraud taking place you should refuse to notarize the document.

This includes someone using an identification card that does not appear to be their own, a document that appears to be fraudulent in nature or that would create a fraudulent transaction or in any other case of fraud.

Example: A young man comes to you to have an affidavit notarized. While you are checking his identification you see a slit in the plastic near the photo and notice that the photograph on the driver's license is raised. Once you notice that his identification appears to be fraudulent or forged you must refuse to notarize the document.

Altered State of Mind

This can be a tricky thing to determine, but if a signer of a document appears be in an altered mental state then you must refuse to notarize the document.

A person with an altered state of mind may not understand the document or what the purpose of the document is. If they do not understand this then they cannot possibly be signing a document "for the purposes stated therein". If you have any doubts about the state of mind of the signer then you can make a good effort to establish their state of mind by asking questions such as "Do you know today's date?, Do you know what this document is for?, Do you know where we are right now?". If you still have doubts as to the state of mind of the signer you must refuse to notarize the document.

An easy example of altered state of mind might be a patient in a hospital. If the patient has recently received a narcotic or other mind altering drug you should refuse to notarize the document. If you are unsure about the state of mind of the patient you can explain to the nurse that you are a notary there in your official capacity and need to know if they feel the patient is in a state of mind to sign legal documents.

A more difficult example might be someone who comes to have a document notarized and appears to be confused or disoriented. When you ask them if they know what the document is and what it's for they should be able to answer. If they give you an answer such as: "I am not sure, my son gave it to me and said I had to come have it notarized." Then you should refuse to notarize or ask them to read the document and then ask them again. If they are still not sure then you must refuse.

Coercion

If a signer of a document appears to be forced or coerced in to signing a document then you should refuse to notarize.

Always ask the person if they are signing the document willingly. If there is a relative or other person present who appears to be pushing to have the document notarized you should ask them to step out of the room and ask the signer again if they feel comfortable signing and if they are being forced or pressured to sign. If they say they don't want to sign or indicate that someone is making them sign then you must refuse.

Criminal Activity

If you have any indication or the signer(s) of a document make any sort of comment that indicates that the document is being used to further a criminal activity then you must refuse to notarize the document.

For instance: if two people come in to have title transfer paperwork notarized and one of them makes a comment alluding to the fact that they are transferring the car title so they can keep the car even though their license to drive has been suspended you must refuse to notarize the document.

Improper Refusals

The following are some of the circumstances in which you may not refuse services to a client. Refusing services under these circumstances may subject you to criminal and civil liability.

Discriminatory Reasons

You must not refuse to notarize a document for any discriminatory purpose including but not limited to race, gender, age (provided they have proper identification), religious beliefs, national origin, political beliefs, sexual orientation, veteran status, disability or marital status.

The 14th Amendment to the United States Constitution guarantees "equal protection of the laws" to any person within the jurisdiction of any state.

> *"No State shall make or enforce any law which shall abridge the privileges or immunities of citizens of the United States; nor shall any State deprive any person of life, liberty, or property, without due process of law; nor deny to any person within its jurisdiction the equal protection of the laws."*

If you discriminate against any person then you are denying them "equal protection" of the law and are "abridging or depriving" the person of the privileges or immunities to which they are entitled as United States citizens. This would also be a violation of your oath of office as a notary; as your oath clearly states that you swear (or affirm) to "preserve, protect and defend the Constitution and laws of the United States and this state."

Also, refusing notary services based on a discriminatory reason is a violation of United States federal law.

> Title 18, U.S.C., Section 242
> Deprivation of Rights Under Color of Law
>
> This statute makes it a crime for any person acting under color of law, statute, ordinance, regulation, or custom to willfully deprive or cause to be deprived from any person those rights, privileges, or immunities secured or protected by the Constitution and laws of the U.S.
>
> This law further prohibits a person acting under color of law, statute, ordinance, regulation or custom to willfully subject or cause to be subjected any person to different punishments, pains, or penalties, than those prescribed for punishment of citizens on account of such person being an alien or by reason of his/her color or race.
>
> Acts under "color of any law" include acts not only done by federal, state, or local officials within the bounds or limits of their lawful authority, but also acts done without and beyond the bounds of their lawful authority; provided that, in order for unlawful acts of any official to be done under "color of any law," the unlawful acts must be done while such official is purporting or pretending to act in the performance of his/her official duties. This definition includes, in addition to law enforcement officials, individuals such as Mayors, Council persons, Judges, Nursing Home Proprietors, Security Guards, etc., persons who are

> bound by laws, statutes ordinances, or customs. (Federal Bureau of Investigation)

You may refuse services to any person when you would normally refuse services to all people. For instance if you take your lunch from 1:00PM to 1:30PM and do not perform notary services during that time period; you may refuse to perform services to any person. Be sure and tell the person when you will be available to help them.

Disagreeing With the Document

You may not refuse notary services simply because you disagree with the contents of the document. Your role is to verify and certify signatures and nothing further. If you disagree with the purpose or result of the document then simply don't do whatever activity it is you disagree with.

The exception to this is if the document will create or further some sort of criminal enterprise. In this circumstance you may refuse notarization.

Chapter 8

Liability and Mitigating Liability

Liability

A notary public is liable for all official acts they perform as well as the failure to perform an act. The notary may face civil, criminal or regulatory penalties for his or her actions.

The best way to limit your exposure to liability is to research and learn as much as you can about notaries and notary law. Take a class, join a notary association and read their publications and newsletters.

Do your best to make sure you act in accordance with the law. Double check your work. After every notarization make sure you entered everything properly in your notary journal. Check the document to make sure that everything has been completed and you signed and stamped the document.

Civil Liability

You may be held civilly liable if another party suffers a financial or other loss due to your actions, errors or omissions.

For example: if you notarize the signatures on a travel document but fail to affix your seal and as a result a family vacation is ruined; you are liable, at minimum, for cost of the lost vacation. The injured party may even be able to recover damages for mental anguish, punitive damages or some other type of damage allowed by law.

Criminal Liability

If you make any false statements on a notary certificate or use your office to commit fraud or to secure favors from another person then you are criminally liable.

Examples of actions that lead to criminal liability:

- Notarizing a document without the signer being personally present
- Making a false statement or listing the wrong date on a notary certificate
- Practicing law without a license
- Advertising as a "notario" or "notario publico"
- Using another notary's stamp
- Signing a notarial certificate with any name other than the name on your notary certificate
- Using your office for personal gain (other than allowed fees)
- Accepting bribes
- Selling confidential information obtained in your official capacity

You must maintain strict ethical and professional standards and must never do anything that will violate those standards. If you ever have an ethical question you should contact the Secretary of State's office.

If you have a specific legal question concerning your official duties you should speak with a licensed attorney or request an opinion from your county attorney or the Secretary of State. You should make your request in writing. Call the respective office to get instructions for requesting a formal opinion.

Regulatory Liability

If you violate any law or regulation pertaining to the office of notary public you may be subject to regulatory liability by the Office of the Secretary of State of Texas.

The Secretary of State is charged with enforcing the notary laws and ensuring the compliance of notaries within the state.

The Secretary of State receives and investigates complaints against notaries public. Upon receipt of a complaint the Secretary of State will initiate an investigation and will proceed with disciplinary actions against the notary involved. The outcome of these proceedings can include sanctions, suspension, revocation or denial of a future commission.

Mitigating Liability

There are several ways of mitigating liability but you will never escape liability for your actions. The best way to avoid liability is to check and double check your work and to not proceed with an official action if you have any doubts or are unsure as to how to proceed.

The purpose of this guide is to give you my opinions and suggestions on how to operate a notary business. I would suggest that you use the "Applicable Laws and Statutes" chapter as a guide and a reference any time you have a question.

Other forms of liability protection include training, insurance and ultimately confidence in what you are doing and the best practice to follow.

Notary Bond

There is a common misconception amongst some notaries that the $10,000.00 notary bond is their protection against any suits or judgments made against them. This is actually quite the opposite.

A bond protects the public and guarantees that any person who has damages as a result of your actions that they can recover at least the face value of the bond, minus any portion already paid out. Once the bond company pays a claim against your bond they will recover those losses from you. If you do not repay voluntarily the bond company will likely file suit against you to recover their losses.

So if your bond company pays a $5,000.00 settlement to a client that is injured by your actions; you will owe the bond company that $5,000.00 and probably some fees.

Errors and Omissions Insurance

Errors and Omissions (E&O) insurance is probably one of the most important products you can buy as a notary public.

Unlike a bond, any E&O policy that you buy will protect you against claims, legal fees and any fines you may be assessed. This type of policy is usually very cheap and on average costs about $12.75 per year per $25,000.00 worth of coverage.

It is best to shop around for coverage and to compare prices. Always read the policy to see what is and is not covered under your policy.

I purchased my policy at www.NotaryRotary.com and got a great deal on it, but again you should shop around and see what's best for you.

Training and Education

Training and education are one of the most effective tools at mitigating losses due to liability. The Texas Secretary of State has published some great training information on their website including a FAQ and a downloadable class that you can take.

In addition to the Texas SOS training I recommend a training course such as the one offered by the American Association of Notaries. You can find a link to it at www.TexasNotary.com. It costs about $25.00 and covers a great deal of information.

While this guide is intended to be a great resource in helping you establish and operate your notary business it is not intended to be a full training manual. One of the best things you can do is to read all of the applicable laws and regulations and visit various notary forums such as www.123notary.com and Notary Rotary.

Always Follow Proper Procedure

You should always follow proper procedure and make a checklist, if necessary, and use it on every notarization you perform. You can find a sample checklist in the "Reference Documents" chapter. Following proper procedures and double checking your work will help you vastly reduce errors.

It is better to double check your work than it is to commit an error. Remember that the papers you will be working with are often important legal and business documents and that a simple mistake can have serious consequences.

If a client asks or appears curious about why I am re-reading everything I simply tell them that I double-check my work while they are still there so that any mistakes can be corrected before they leave. I don't want to be the cause of a document being rejected or unenforceable and you shouldn't either.

Chapter 9

Procedure

You should develop and follow a proper procedure for notarizing documents or for any other official acts you perform.

Check Photo Identification

The first thing you do should be to check the signer's photo identification. Requirements for identification in the state of Texas are as follows:

- Must be issued by any US state or the United States Federal Government (A foreign passport is acceptable for real estate transactions only)
- Must be unexpired
- Must have a photograph
- Must have a serial number
- Must have a physical description
- Must have a copy of the person's signature

Note: You may notarize a document for someone who is personally known to you without verifying their identification. The person must be known to you and not just someone who you know casually. You may also accept the oath of a credible witness, who is personally known to you, to establish the identity of a signer.

Record the Signer's Information in the Journal

Immediately after reviewing the person's identification (or while you are reviewing it) you should record their information in your journal.

You should do this before reviewing the document so that you will have the necessary information already recorded on the chance that you may need to refuse services.

If there is more than one document signer make a separate journal entry for each person who will be signing. Be sure and indicate that they are additional signers on the same document.

Review the Document to be Notarized

Skim through the document to make sure there are no blank spaces, to get an idea of the general purpose of the document and to verify the names of the document signer(s).

Perform the Verbal Ceremony and Client Signing

The verbal ceremony is absolutely vital to any notarization. If you do not perform the verbal ceremony then you have not notarized the document and you have made a false statement on the notary certificate.

If the notary certificate says "acknowledged before me" or "sworn to", etc... and you have not asked them to acknowledge or swear to the document then how can you have truthfully completed the notarial certificate?

Remember that completing a notarial certificate indicating that you have done something that you have not done not only invalidates the notarization but could lead to criminal perjury charges being filed against you.

Acknowledgment

If you are notarizing the signatures on an acknowledgment or proof; the document can or will be signed prior to coming to you for notarization. For this type of notarization this is acceptable as you are asking the signer(s) to acknowledge their signature.

If the document is not signed have the signer sign it before proceeding to the verbal ceremony. They cannot acknowledge their signature if they have not signed the document.

The verbal ceremony for an acknowledgment is relatively straightforward and will be along the lines of "Do you acknowledge that this is your signature, that you signed the document willingly and that you signed it for the purposes stated therein?"

Oath or Affirmation

If the notary certificate includes the phrase "sworn" then you will be placing the signer(s) under oath. This is called an oath or affirmation.

For this type of notarization the document must not have been signed prior to being notarized. If the signer has already signed the document you must have them sign it again in your presence immediately above where they have already signed. Do not have them sign (or re-sign) the document until after you have performed the verbal ceremony.

Example:

The following is the oath of office for a notary public in the state of Texas:

> I, ________________, do solemnly swear (or affirm), that I will faithfully execute the duties of the office of notary public of the State of Texas, and will to the best of my ability preserve, protect and defend the Constitution and laws of the United States and this state, so help me God.

To administer the oath of office for a notary public named John Doe you will ask him to raise his right hand, to indicate that he is taking an oath, and ask the following:

"Do you, John Doe, solemnly swear or affirm that you will faithfully execute the duties of the office of notary public of the State of Texas and that you will to the best of your ability preserve, protect and defend the Constitution and the laws of the United States and of this state, so help you God?"

You must receive a verbal answer in the affirmative such as "yes" or "I do".

Have the Signer Sign the Document and Certificate

The next step is to ask the signer to sign the document, if necessary, and the notary certificate.

If the document was already signed before coming to you then have the signer re-sign the document immediately above where they previously signed. If this happens you should write "Duplicate signature affixed at notary's request" to indicate to anyone reading the document that you requested the duplicate signature. You should also make a note of this in your notary journal.

Have the Signer Sign Your Journal

After the verbal ceremony is complete and the signer(s) have signed the document you should have the sign your journal as well. This is helps prove the validity of your journal entry and of the notary act you have performed.

A person taking an oath or making an acknowledgment is not required to sign your journal. However, you should tell them that you ask for the signature to help prove that it was actually them who had the document notarized.

Thumbprint

The Texas Secretary of State recommends that you do not ask for copies of thumbprints for your journal entries, but does not prohibit it.

I always ask the signer(s) to provide a copy of their thumbprint but tell them that it is not required and that it just helps prove that they signed the document if it is ever called in to question.

The way I look at it is that someone may be able to claim that their identity was stolen and their signature forged both on a document and in your journal but they cannot claim that their thumb was stolen (well I guess if one is missing they can) and used in your journal.

I recommend asking for the thumbprint to protect yourself and the interests of the document signer. If someone notarizes a document they do so for whatever reason is stated in the document; this is proved by the verbal ceremony where they indicate that they signed it, they signed it willingly and they signed it for the purposes stated therein (or they swore to the truthfulness of the contents). If someone claims after the signers death or after the signer becomes incapacitated that they signature is not valid then you will now also have the signer's thumbprint in your journal indicating that (s)he did sign the document.

This is a decision that you have to make and not one that I can or should make for you.

Also be advised there is a law in the State of Texas concerning the collection of biometric information for a commercial purpose. A notary is an officer of the state so any information collected is not for a commercial purpose, but for a governmental purpose.

Complete the Notary Certificate

The next step is to complete and sign the notary certificate. Some notaries prefer to just fill in the blanks and sign while others prefer to edit the certificate appropriately.

I recommend editing the certificate so that it most accurately reflects what took place. Editing the certificate makes the certificate look more professional but also removes any doubts that may arise. For instance if the certificate says both personally known to you and says proved through an ID and you have not crossed one out; which is it? Was the signer personally known? Did you check their ID? Did you personally know the signer and check their ID?

Example:

You are located in Lubbock County and are John Doe, Notary Public. A client, John Smith, comes to you with a document that needs to be notarized and includes an ordinary certificate of acknowledgment. This client is not known to you so you verify his identity through his US Passport.

You would complete the notary certificate as follows:

The State of Texas
County of Lubbock

Before me John Doe, Notary Public (here insert the name and character of the officer) on this day personally appeared John Smith, ~~known to me (or~~ proved to me ~~on the oath of ________________ or~~ through a United States Passport (description of identity card or other document)) to be the person whose name is subscribed to the foregoing instrument and acknowledged to me that he executed the same for the purposes and consideration therein expressed.

(Seal) Given under my hand and seal of office this 26th day of September, A.D., 2013.

John Doe

Notary Public, State of Texas

The certificate now reads that John Smith personally appeared before you and that you proved his identity through a United States Passport.

Double-Check the Document and Certificate

The next thing you should do, before you affix your seal to authenticate the notarization, is to double-check everything. This is where your checklist may come in handy. Make sure the venue is completed, make sure you have dated and signed the certificate, and make sure your journal entry is complete.

This may also be a good time to collect your fee and issue a receipt if you have any doubts as to whether they will pay.

Affix Your Seal

A notarial act is not complete without a notary seal. This seal is what lets the recipient of the document know that the document was officially notarized and not just signed by someone in a dark alley behind K-Mart pretending to be a notary.

I recommend this as the final part of the notarization; because once your seal is affixed, you have notarized the document. If there are no errors you have notarized it correctly and within the confines of law. If there is an error or mistake you have incorrectly or illegally notarized the document.

Chapter 10

Special Circumstances

There will be times when you will face a situation that is out of the ordinary or that requires special care and consideration. It is best to learn about and familiarize yourself with these potential situations so that if you are ever confronted with one of them you will be prepared and ready to go.

I-9 Employment Eligibility Verification

At some point you will undoubtedly be asked to complete or verify an I-9 form to verify the eligibility for a person to work in the United States.

It is extremely important to understand that an I-9 form does NOT require notarization and that you are forbidden by the Texas Secretary of State from notarizing these documents.

With that being said, you can still complete these forms as a service to the employer.

Authorized Representative

If an employer needs to have an I-9 form completed for a new-hire you may act as an "Authorized Representative" for the employer. You must make it absolutely clear that you will act as an authorized representative only and will not acting in your capacity as a notary public.

You should have the employer send you an email or fax designating you as an authorized representative and granting you the authority to review and verify identity and work authorization documents on their behalf.

Make sure you negotiate your fee with the employer prior to meeting with an employee. If this type of arrangement is done properly it can be quite profitable for your business. Never use your notary seal on an I-9 form or any accompanying paperwork.

Billing

Make it absolutely clear on your invoices, statements and receipts that this is a non-notary service that you offer. Just as photocopying services are not notary services, authorized representative services are not notary services.

Signing Document for an Individual With a Disability

You may be called to notarize a document for an individual with a disability who is unable to sign or make a mark on the document to be notarized. The disability must be physical in nature and not caused by mental incapacity as a person who lacks mental capacity to sign a document is unable to verify that they signed the document willingly and for the reasons stated in the document.

You are specifically authorized by Section 406.0165 of the Texas Government Code to sign the name of the person with a disability to a document to be notarized if:

- The individual with a disability requests you to do so
- A disinterested witness is present. The witness must have no interest in the document or the outcome of the document or to any property affected by the document.

If you affix a person's signature to a document under this section of law you must:

- You must check the identification of the witness and record their name and residential address in your journal as you would a witness to any other document

- You must write the following sentence, or a substantially similar one, beneath the signature you have affixed
    - "Signature affixed by notary in the presence of (name of witness), a disinterested witness, under Section 406.0165, Government Code."

You then proceed to notarize the document as you normally would. Your journal entry should indicate that you affixed the signature in accordance with TX. Govt Code 406.0165.

A signature affixed in this manner has the same effect as if the signer signed the document themselves.

Please note that the verbal ceremony must still be completed and that this section only applies to individuals who are disabled and physically unable to sign. This does not apply to people who just don't want to sign such as someone who just put lotion on their hands or for any other non-disability reason.

Notarizing Foreign Language Documents

You may receive a request to notarize a document in a language other than English. It is perfectly legal for you to notarize this document so long as you can still verify there are no blank spaces or missing information, verify the names of signers or any other information you would normally look for in an English language document.

Notary Certificate

No matter the language of the document the notary certificate must be completed in English. You are not allowed to notarize a non-English notary certificate.

Communication With Signer

You must be able to communicate directly with the signer. You cannot rely on a translator or interpreter to assist you in performing the verbal ceremony. You can communicate in writing or in verbally. If you communicate in writing consider keeping a copy in your notarial records.

Notarizing for a Deaf or Hearing Impaired Individual

If you are requested to notarize a document for a deaf or hearing impaired individual you may communicate in writing. You may accept a head nod as an answer to a verbal question. For instance, if the individual can read lips you proceed with the verbal ceremony as usual. If the person nods their head in the affirmative you may take that as a "yes" to your question.

If you communicate in writing consider keeping a copy of the written communications in your notarial records. Be sure and note the circumstances of the notarization in your journal.

Notarizing for a Blind or Visually Impaired Person

You may notarize a document for a blind or visually impaired person; but you must read the entire document to them, word for word. You may not explain the document or the meaning of its contents.

You are required to read the document to the signer. It is unacceptable for you to assume that the person who drafted the document has fully explained the document to the signer prior to their meeting with you.

After reading the document to the signer proceed with the verbal ceremony and the signing of the document. You may direct their hand to the proper place on the document for them to sign.

Signature by Mark

If you have a signer who is illiterate or otherwise unable to sign their name they may do so by making a mark on the document.

You must establish that the person signing the document understands the document and that they know what they are signing for. If they do not understand you must refuse the notarization and refer them to a licensed attorney.

If you are satisfied that they have the understanding and capacity to sign the document then you may have them place an "X" on the signature line. After they place their mark you write the first name before and last name after the mark, or have them place a mark on a line titled “His Mark” or “Her Mark” with their name written below it.

You must then have a disinterested witness sign the document as well. The witness information should be verified and recorded in your journal just as you would any other witness.

I have included sample notary certificates for signature by mark in the Reference and Sample Documents chapter.

Chapter 11

Depositions and Subpoenas

Depositions and subpoenas are tools used to gather information for litigation. Most of the time these types of scenarios will be handled by an attorney or one of their staff members. However, you should be aware that a notary public has the authority to take depositions and to issue subpoenas.

Depositions

A deposition is a method by which an attorney or person that is a party to litigation gathers information before a trial or other court proceeding to use during the proceeding. Witnesses are usually deposed before testifying in court.

A notary has the authority to swear a witness to a deposition and to verify their answers to the deposition. The notary does not decide what questions to ask but simply verifies the answers with the person being deposed.

A person representing themselves my hire a notary to take the deposition as that person may not be authorized by law to take a deposition.

Subpoenas

As I mentioned earlier, subpoenas are powerful legal tools used to compel the production of documents or other evidence and to compel the attendance of a witness at a deposition or other hearing.

A notary is authorized to issue subpoenas to compel attendance at a deposition or to compel a witness to a document to appear before the notary to prove the document.

Subpoena for Proof of Document

If a witness to a document refuses or fails to appear before an officer of the state authorized to take a proof of a document then that officer may issue a subpoena requiring the appearance of the witness.

Section 121.013(a) and (b) of the Texas Civil Practice and Remedies Code state:

(a) On the sworn application of a person interested in the proof of an instrument required or permitted by law to be recorded, stating that a witness to the instrument refuses to appear and testify regarding the execution of the instrument and that the instrument cannot be proven without the evidence of the witness, an officer authorized to take proofs of instruments shall issue a subpoena requiring the witness to appear before the officer and testify about the execution of the instrument.

(b) If the witness fails to obey the subpoena, the officer has the same powers to enforce the attendance and compel the answers of the witness as does a district judge. Attachment may not be issued, however, unless the witness receives or is tendered the same compensation that is made to witnesses in other cases. An officer may not require the witness to leave his county of residence, but if the witness is temporarily present in the county where the execution of the

> instrument is sought to be proven for registration, he may be required to appear.

Failure to obey a lawfully issued subpoena will result in fines or jail time for contempt of court. If you issue a subpoena and the recipient does not respond you should speak with the district court clerk or with the district attorney's office.

Subpoena for Deposition

Just as a notary may issue a subpoena to compel a witness to testify to prove a document a notary may issue a subpoena to compel testimony at a deposition. As stated earlier these types of proceedings are usually handled by an attorney's office but you may come across a situation where a litigant is representing themselves in court and hires you to conduct the deposition.

As with the issuance of a subpoena to prove a document there are strict requirements for the issuance of a subpoena to compel testimony at a deposition.

Rule 176.4(c) of the Texas Rules of Civil Procedure specifically authorizes any person authorized to take depositions to issue a subpoena for a deposition.

> an officer authorized to take depositions in this State, who must issue the subpoena immediately on a request accompanied by a notice to take a deposition under Rules 199 or 200, or a notice under Rule 205.3, and who may also serve the notice with the subpoena. (Texas Supreme Court, 2014)

Before issuing a subpoena under this or any other chapter or rule you should research and study the applicable laws to ensure you are in compliance such rule or chapter of law.

Chapter 12

Electronic Notarizations

Texas state law allows the electronic notarization of any document that would otherwise be eligible to be notarized.

Requirements

Electronic notarizations must meet the same basic requirements as a standard notarization; you must log the notarization in a log book and a seal meeting the same size and design requirements as a regular notary stamp must be affixed to or associated with the document and must be reproduced when printed.

You must continue to demand personal appearance and you must verify the identity of each signer. These requirements do not change just because the notarization is electronic.

Journal

In addition to electronic notarization you may keep an electronic notary journal so long as it meets the same basic requirements as a standard journal.

One thing to keep in mind is that you must have access to your electronic notary journal so long as you remain a commissioned notary public. After your commission expires, and you do not seek renewal, or after it is revoked you must provide a copy of your electronic journal and all of its contents to your county clerk just as you would your regular journal.

Chapter 13

Protecting Yourself, Safety and Security

Protecting yourself and maintaining your own safety and security and the security of your office is of utmost importance.

This chapter will focus on protecting you from the actions of others and how those actions can negatively impact your business and your safety.

These suggestions are only precautionary but I do think it is prudent to hope for the best and plan for the worst.

Physical Security

Implementing safety conscious procedures and practices is essential to operating any successful business. Here are some tips and pointers that can help you develop your own security plan.

Cash Handling

You should limit the amount of cash you keep on hand and definitely restrict the amount of cash you ever display to a customer. I usually keep about $20.00 in change on me at any given time so that I can make change for a $6.00 transaction. A display of large amounts of cash, especially with someone who operates a primarily mobile business, is dangerous.

I also accept checks, credit and debit cards. My bank allows me to electronically deposit checks from my smart phone. I also use Square Register and Flint Mobile to accept credit and debit cards respectively. The fees are minimal and accepting credit and debit cards is all but required in modern society.

Let Someone Know Where You Will Be

If you are operating as a mobile notary then make sure you let someone know where you will be at all times. If you accept an appointment to meet someone at their home, business or other location let a friend or family member know what the address is and the approximate appointment times.

If possible or practical try to meet the client at a neutral place such as Starbucks or McDonalds or some other location. The downside to this is that privacy will be limited. Another option is to take someone with you if that makes you feel more comfortable.

Use a Mobile Security App

There are several apps available for Android and iPhone that you can use in an emergency to let someone know your exact location (GPS based) and that you need assistance.

This could prove beneficial not only for a mechanical problem with your car but also if you encounter some sort of hostile situation while on an appointment. Examples of these apps include SOS-Stay Safe and One Touch SOS.

These can be activated by pressing a button on your phone or some other discreet action so that you can activate the system without letting anyone around you know that you have done so.

Data Security

Data security is vital for any modern business. As a notary public you will, at times, be entrusted to extremely sensitive and confidential information of the clients you serve. You must develop and implement a data security plan to ensure that you are taking the required steps to protect your client's data.

Mobile Data Security

Norton Mobile Security is another app you can download for iPhone and Android. Norton Mobile Security has several features to help you locate and secure a lost or stolen cell phone.

Most people have a tremendous amount of personal data on their phones, sometimes without realizing just how much is stored on the phone.

Our phones provide access to all sorts of data sources such as email, text messaging, banking and credit card apps, social media, medical and pharmacy data and so much. Now factor in a mobile business where you will be receiving emails and messages from clients and processing client payments and you have a ton of personal data that you must safeguard.

It is bad enough if your own data is lost, but it is a very bad situation if you possess someone else's data and it is lost or compromised.

Norton Mobile Security has many remote functions to help you manage your phone and maintain the integrity of your data security.

Features of Norton Mobile Security:

- Remote lock
    - Allows you to remotely lock your phone from any computer with internet access or via text command. When this feature is activated a lock screen will appear on your phone with any custom text you wish to include. Also your phone will start transmitting it's GPS coordinates to your secure Norton account and will activate it's camera in regular intervals to try and get a picture of whoever may now be in possession of your phone.
- Remote scream
    - No matter what volume level your ringer is on if you send the remote scream command your phone will emit a loud alarm type tone to help you find it. I tend to keep my phone on vibrate while with a client or somewhere such as a doctor's office. This feature

allows me to find my phone if I lose it. This can also be used to draw attention to your phone if it is stolen.

- Remote locate
  - In the event your phone is lost or stolen you can activate the remote locate function. Your phone will transmit its GPS coordinates to your secure Norton website and will also activate the camera as with the remote lock function.
- Remote wipe
  - This feature will remotely wipe all data from your device in the event it is stolen. If you have sensitive client documents on your phone and you know it has been stolen you can use this do remotely active a factory data reset of your device.

Computer Data Security

You should make every effort to secure and encrypt any sensitive or confidential client files that you may have stored on your computer.

While any files you keep as a notary are technically public information you still have a duty to secure those files and only disclose the information in accordance with a signed request for a copy.

Any files that you keep outside of your capacity as a notary public, such as any copies of the identity documents used in I-9 Employment Eligibility Verifications, are not subject to public disclosure and must be secured.

I keep a client files folder on my computer. Inside of that folder I make a folder for each client. Within the client folder I have two folders; one labeled “Notary Files” and one labeled “Non-Notary Files”. I use two folders to show a clear distinction between official notary records and non-notary business records.

Each folder is encrypted so that even if someone gains access to my computer they cannot access the folders. This not only prohibits unauthorized access to the data but also unauthorized modification or removal of data.

Physical Data Security

You should keep any paper notary public records in a safe place where they will be free from unauthorized access by any person. This also applies to your notary journal and any old notary journals you have in your possession. You must keep these under lock and key so as to maintain the integrity of the data.

Remember, as a notary public, you are required to safeguard your notary journals and files as official governmental records.

Texas Penal Code Section 37.10(a)(1) makes it a crime to make a false alteration to a governmental record.

Texas Penal Code Section 37.10(a)(4) makes it a crime to possess a governmental record unlawfully. A notary may possess his or her records in their official capacity, so it is lawful. It is unlawful for any other person, including a friend or relative, to possess those records.

Acts Against the Notary

It is not very common, but there are times when a person may attempt to bribe or coerce a notary public in order to have a document notarized or in order to get the notary to perform an act outside of their legal authorities; such as not checking valid identification before notarizing a document. These are serious crimes.

While you can never anticipate one of these situations, you must be prepared to deal with one if it arises.

Bribery

There may be an instance where someone will attempt to offer you a higher fee, money or some other thing or service of value in order that you "bend the rules" for them. Make no mistake about it, this is bribery. It is a crime to either offer or accept a bribe.

Texas Penal Code Section 36.02 makes it a second degree felony to offer or accept a bribe to influence a public servant's decision with regards to their official duties or in connection with any judicial or administrative proceeding.

> (a) A person commits an offense if he intentionally or knowingly offers, confers, or agrees to confer on another, or solicits, accepts, or agrees to accept from another:
>
> (1) any benefit as consideration for the recipient's decision, opinion, recommendation, vote, or other exercise of discretion as a public servant, party official, or voter;
>
> (2) any benefit as consideration for the recipient's decision, vote, recommendation, or other exercise of official discretion in a judicial or administrative proceeding;

If someone offers you a bribe, in any manner, you must refuse to accept and you should refuse to offer any notary services to that person. In addition, you should immediately report the incident to the local police and make sure you get a copy of the police report.

If this person later attempts to claim that you did accept a bribe you will need documentation that not only did you refuse it, but you immediately contacted law enforcement.

Coercion

Coercion is the threat or use of violence or force to influence the decision of a public servant in the exercise of their official duties. If you can safely escape the situation you should do so immediately and call 911 or another police emergency line.

If you are unable to escape the situation and you feel that you are in danger you should comply with the person's request; if you feel it will protect your safety. As soon as the person leaves, or you are able to escape the situation, you should immediately call 911 or another police emergency line and lock the doors to prohibit the offender from returning.

Your safety is your first and most important priority. Do not do anything that might lead to the person harming you.

If you completed an official act while under threat of violence or other harm you should immediately forward any police report to the Secretary of State so they will have a record of the act.

Also, if you are able to remember any identifying information about the person or the document you should make those details available to the police and the Secretary of State.

For instance; if you were coerced into notarizing a child support affidavit by a white male appearing to be 40 to 45 years old for use in a specific court, you should make these details available to the police and that court.

Another suggestion, if you are in the state of mind to think of this during the situation, is to make some sort of alteration to the notary certificate to distinguish it from a normal notarization you conduct.

For example; your name is John Michael Doe but your commission is in the name John Doe and you always sign the notary certificate as John Doe (as required by law); you may want to sign a coerced notary certificate as J. M. Doe or John M. Doe. If you do this you can then notify the court and the police that you always sign certificates as John Doe but you signed this one in a different manner to distinguish it from a valid notarization. This way the police and the court can be on the look-out for a document with your notary stamp but with a distinguished signature.

In case of either bribery or coercion you must notify the police immediately. Notifying the police will not only help ensure your safety but will also help ensure the integrity of your office as notary public. This would also be a good time to activate your SOS program on your phone.

Favors for Friends and Family

Texas Notary Law does not prohibit you from notarizing documents for friends or family but you must not allow that personal relationship to interfere with your judgment or responsibility as a notary public.

For instance you cannot make an exception to the personal appearance requirement just because you know or are related to the person. You must treat the notarial act no different than you would for a member of the general public. You are not required to charge any fees, but if you do you must still be ready to issue a receipt.

Also keep in mind that you may not notarize a document in which you have an interest. For example; if your cousin is transferring property to your mother, you should not notarize any of the transfer paperwork as you have an interest in your mother's estate.

Chapter 14

Starting Your Business

Now that we have covered how to become a notary public and the various aspects of your official duties as a notary we will discuss how to start and operate your business and some best business practices. In this chapter we'll discuss business structure, business registration and taxes. Please note, you should consult with an attorney or tax consultant for specific information that you may need. The information here is just a guide and not a substitute for legal or tax advice.

Business Structure

The first thing to do when opening a new business is to decide on a business structure. Will you incorporate? Are you forming a partnership? Will you operate as a sole proprietorship?

Sole Proprietorship

A sole proprietorship is the simplest and easiest business structure you can choose. Income taxes are much easier and there is less paperwork involved.

A sole proprietorship is a business that is fully owned by a person and whose finances and taxes are intertwined with the owner. Unlike a corporation you do not need to file a separate income tax return or file all of those reports and hold corporate meetings, etc...

Also a sole proprietorship does not have to register and file franchise taxes in Texas.

Corporation

When you form a corporation you are creating a legal entity. As a separate legal entity; a corporation must file its own tax returns and other documents and reports.

Corporate law is complex and if you decide to incorporate then you should consult an attorney for advice and to draft the articles of incorporation.

A general benefit of a corporation is that in most circumstances it, as a separate legal entity, provides some level of liability protection for its owners.

However, you should note that Texas law is very specific in stating that a notary commission is issued to a person and not a company and that a notary is personally responsible for all notarial acts they perform.

Forming a corporation will not alleviate any personal liabilities you have as a notary public, but may alleviate some of the personal liability associated with non-notarial business activities. You should consult an attorney for more information.

Partnership

Another business structure you can choose from is that of a partnership. A partnership operates much in the same way as a corporation except that instead of shareholders a partnership is owned by one or more persons as partners.

Choosing a Business Name

After you decide on the legal structure of your business you should choose a name for your business. You can choose to operate under your own name or an assumed name.

Whatever name you choose it should be professional and convey your business services to others. For instance; if you live in Kempner you may choose a name such as Kempner Notary or Kempner Notary and Business Services.

Assumed Name Certificate

After you choose a business name you should file an assumed name certificate with your County Clerk. This certificate is required to operate a business under any name other than your own. Once you file the certificate and it is approved you may begin using your chosen business name.

Open Tax Accounts

Now that you have chosen a business structure and officially selected and secured a name you should open the appropriate tax accounts with the state and federal governments.

IRS Tax ID Number

You may want to consider applying for a Tax Identification Number or EIN from the IRS. If you incorporate or chose a partnership you may be required to apply for an EIN or Taxpayer Identification Number.

If you will have employees or hire contract labor you will need an EIN.

No matter which business structure you choose, I would recommend getting the EIN; you will probably need it to open a business checking account or any other type of business account, such as gas cards, etc….

Texas Sales and Use Tax Permit

You should apply for a Texas Sales and Use Tax Permit before you begin operations as a notary. Notary public services are not subject to sales or use tax but many of the other services you will likely be offering are subject to these taxes. You must have the permit to collect the taxes.

Examples of taxable services that you may be providing include:

- Copying and fax service
- Data processing
- Printing services

A list of taxable services can be found at the following website http://www.window.state.tx.us/taxinfo/taxpubs/tx96_259.pdf.

If you are unsure whether or not a service you provide or plan to provide is taxable you should call the Texas Comptroller of Public Accounts for clarification.

Texas Workforce Commission (Unemployment)

If you plan to hire employees or contract labor you may need to register with the Texas Workforce Commission to see if you are required to pay unemployment taxes.

Open Business Banking Accounts

Next you may want to consider opening a business checking account. You will need your EIN number to open the account. If you are running a sole proprietorship then you can use your personal checking account if you wish. However; if you are operating as a corporation or a partnership you will need to open a business account.

One of the benefits to having a business account is that it will separate your personal and business finances. You can always write yourself a check when you are ready to be paid.

A benefit to using just your personal account is lower bank fees.

If you plan on hiring employees or contracting work to other notaries you should consider a separate checking account for your business.

Write a Standard Operating Procedure

No matter your business structure it is important to write out a Standard Operating Procedure (SOP). There is no requirement that you have one of these but it is a good idea, especially if you will have employees or contract labor.

The two primary reasons for a SOP are to ensure consistency and to have a written policy to use as a reference when you need guidance on how you should proceed in a particular situation.

This is especially vital if you have any employees as this will help ensure your business will offer consistent service each and every time.

The key to a SOP is making sure that it is followed at all times and updated or modified as needed.

Chapter 15

Advertising and Marketing

Developing and instituting a viable marketing plan is vital for all businesses, especially new businesses. As a new business you don't have an existing client base so every client will be a new client. You will need an action plan to attract new clients.

Internet Advertising

If you want to attract customers you will have to advertise online. There is almost no way to open a new business and be successful without an online presence.

Website

You will need a website and email. You need to come up with a professional and simple web address. If at all possible get a .com address. I personally find the .us and .biz addresses to be less professional than a .com.

There are several hosting and web design companies you can choose from. I have used both GoDaddy.com and 1and1.com. I currently use 1 and 1 because of the simplicity and ease of use of their systems.

GoDaddy may be a little better if you plan on having your website professionally designed or designed via software on your computer.

If at all possible your website should offer online scheduling and other features that will appeal to busy people. Remember: mobile notary is a service of convenience. The more convenient you make it to schedule services the more likely you will be used.

Listing Services

There are several online listing services available that will list your company with various search engines, map and GPS providers, business directories and review sites.

You should list your business and website with one of these providers as soon as possible. The sooner you list with one of these companies the sooner people will be able to find you online. Customers will likely be searching the web for a notary public when the need arises for them to have a document notarized. Not being listed will cost a lot of business that you cannot afford to lose.

ExpressUpdates.com and Yext.com are two good listing service providers who both offer good products.

Consumer Review Sites

Consumer review sites are gaining popularity. Many people check these sites to find physicians, daycares, plumbers, mechanics and all sorts of other services they need for their home and business.

There are two main benefits to listing yourself with review sites: they are another avenue for people to find your services and they provide a source of feedback for your business. Good feedback is a great tool at attracting customers and poor feedback will show you the areas of your operations that need improvement.

I regularly check Angie's List and Yelp for reviews of services that I need and I review businesses I visit on both.

Craigslist

Free advertising is always good advertising. You may want to post an ad to Craigslist. Many people, especially younger people, check Craigslist for almost everything.

You may or may not get a result but either way you won't pay anything to advertise so you won't be out any money even if it does not yield any business.

Social Media

As long as you can avoid posting something hideously bad that goes viral; social media is an excellent way to connect with others in the community.

Facebook

Facebook is a great place to list your business. Creating and maintaining a Facebook page will help you stay connected with the community and with your clients.

Facebook is also a great place to list specials and post various articles. If you are able to post things that bring interest from others your reach will expand. Expanded reach is expanded business.

Twitter

Twitter is an extraordinarily powerful social media platform. Twitter allows you to "follow" people (and not get charged with stalking) and allows people to follow you.

When you follow someone any message they send out, called a tweet, appears on your timeline. Anything you tweet will show up on your followers' timelines as well.

Twitter is a great place to find people and send out messages of up to 140 characters each. You can also follow other businesses on twitter and do some business networking.

Foursquare

Foursquare is a location based social media platform. Any time you visit a place that is listed on Foursquare you can "check-in" to that place. Checking-in somewhere allows your friends on Foursquare to see where you are. Foursquare can also link to Facebook and Twitter so a check-in on Foursquare may be transmitted via Twitter and Facebook as well.

If you list your business on Foursquare and someone checks-in at your office then that check-in may automatically reach hundreds or thousands of people instantaneously; which will in turn spread your name to others.

Marketing to Other Businesses

Other businesses can be a lucrative source of business for notaries and mobile notaries in general. If you can develop business relationships with other businesses you will do well.

Convenience and availability are essential for attracting customers, but this is especially true with business customers. Make yourself as convenient as possible and work hours to fit other people's schedules.

One thing I do as a convenience to business customers is offer them charge accounts. A business customer can call me up and have a document notarized and I send them a bill at the end of the month. This way they don't have to fish around for cash or take the extra time out to write a check on the spot.

Chamber of Commerce

It may be a good idea for you to join your local Chamber of Commerce. The Chamber of Commerce gives you a great venue to network with other business owners and managers.

This can be an invaluable source of business and referrals.

Remember, convenience is key to attracting business clients. Most business owners and managers can get free notary services from the bank; but they have to leave their business to go down there and only during business hours. You can market your mobile notary service to these same people and market that you can come to them on their schedule.

Pharmacies

Local pharmacies can be a great place to find notary business. Each year every pharmacy in Texas must inventory certain drugs and those drug inventories must be notarized.

It is much more convenient for a notary to come to a pharmacy than it is for the pharmacist-in-charge to go to the notary. A pharmacy cannot operate to any reasonable degree if the pharmacist is not on the premises.

You should stop by and introduce yourself to the owners or pharmacy managers of all of the pharmacies in your community. Be sure and leave a few business cards.

Hospitals

Hospitals can be a good place to find mobile notary clients. There are times when someone may be critically ill or injured and may require the services of a notary.

This may come off a little like an ambulance chaser, but there is no comparison. Chances are if someone is critically ill or injured they may need the services of a notary without delay. These types of visits may be time critical.

Imagine being ill or having been in an accident and needing a major operation. Now imagine that you have not had a living will, healthcare directive or other such document prepared and notarized. The hospital social worker can provide the forms but not the notary services. This is where you come in. Having these matters taken care of before surgery or extensive medical care can be huge relief for the patient and provide peace of mind.

You might want to stop by your community hospitals and speak with the social workers and charge nurses and provide copies of your business cards.

Jails

People who are incarcerated my need the services of a notary for a variety of reasons such as power of attorney documents, court papers, child custody and guardianship papers and much more. These people are also literally a "captive audience".

You can visit the local jails and leave your information with the guards in the visiting area. If someone approaches them asking about notary services they may pass your information along.

You may also consider writing the warden or administrative offices as well.

Please note: Inmates must have proper identification for you to notarize a document. Chances are that you will be contacted by a friend or family member who will actually hire and pay you. If you get a call for mobile notary services at a jail make sure the caller has the valid identification card in their hand and that this person will meet you at the jail. You must also keep in mind that you will have to see the inmate in person, and not via a video conferencing system. This may mean that you will have to enter the secured area of the jail to see the inmate.

You should treat all clients, incarcerated or not, with respect and dignity.

Attorney's Offices

Most attorneys are notaries or they have staff members who are notaries but they may still occasionally need the services of a mobile notary or a notary who is available after-hours.

While out and about you should visit with some local attorney's offices and leave your information should they ever need your services. After all, homebound and incarcerated people may need the services of attorneys and notaries at some point.

Senior Centers

Another place where you can find some potential clients is at senior centers. Seniors may have mobility impairments or difficulty finding transportation to get to a notary.

Medical Clinics

Another great potential source of clients are medical and dental clinics. The various physicians and dentists may occasionally need the services of a notary and just like a pharmacy it is much more convenient if the notary can come to them.

Also, these physicians may have patients in need of mobile notary services.

Travel Agencies

Travel agents will have clients that may need certain travel documents notarized either for themselves or for children that may be traveling with them.

Schools and Church Organizations

Many school and church groups and clubs will plan trips either within the country or abroad that may require forms to be notarized that allow minor children to travel with another adult.

Generally these forms will need to be notarized by both parents.

One thing you can do to save a little time is try to notarize all of the forms for the group at one time, such as at a group meeting.

Car Dealerships

Car dealerships may need the services of a notary from time to time. If a dealer is trying to close a sale and needs a notary right away they may be willing to pay for the services of a mobile notary.

Staffing Agencies

Staffing agencies may need to the services of a notary occasionally to have certain employment forms and contracts notarized.

Car Impound Lots

Another potential source of business are car impound lots. They may have a need for notary services when dealing with titles and other paperwork related to their business activities.

Legal Service Companies

Legal service companies often need notaries in areas all over the country. These companies usually help corporations and attorney's offices with contacting witnesses or other people related to litigation and obtaining affidavits and other legal documents.

You should search online for a list of legal service companies and contact as many as possible to let them know they can call you if they need notary services in your area.

Printed Advertising

Printed Advertising can be just as effective as, and in some instances more effective than, online and electronic advertising. Delivering printed advertising pieces such as business cards, flyers, door hangers and calendars can go a long way towards developing a client base.

Business Cards

You should find high-quality but affordable business cards and have at least 500 printed. The more people you exchange cards with or the more you leave out in various places the larger your potential client base becomes.

VistaPrint.com has some really nice card templates and usually has some great sales going. They print brochures, door hangers, business cards, magnetic car decals and all sorts of other advertising and promotional items.

Your business cards should be clean, elegant and high quality. You are offering a professional service and your cards should reflect your professionalism.

Try and make it a point to give a business card out each time you notarize a document. Let them know they can call you with any questions of if they need something else notarized.

Door Hangers

Door hangers can be another beneficial form of advertising. You should try to avoid taping stuff to people's doors as it leaves a residue that the person then has to clean off.

Door hangers just hang on the knob or handle and are mess free. They can be used to list hours, services, phone numbers, etc....

If you are out performing mobile notary services somewhere take a few minutes and hand some of these on doors in the neighborhood.

Flyers

You can also have some flyers printed up and distribute them at fairs, business expos and other events where people gather.

Magnetic Business Cards

Sometimes magnetic business cards will come in very handy. People are often looking for magnets to hold up papers and receipts and children's artwork, etc... on their fridges.

Some businesses also keep magnets on their fridges, file cabinets, etc... When they need a document notarized they may come across your business card magnet and call you.

Calendars

Calendars are a great advertising tool. If you give someone a calendar, and they use it, they will come across your business info all year long.

Be sure and get a calendar that can be easily written on so people will be more likely to keep and use it.

Public Relations

This might seem like an odd place to put information relating to public relations but good PR does a lot to get your name and business information out to the community.

You might consider volunteering your services somewhere in the community.

For instance your local senior center may have an upcoming workshop teach seniors how to draft their own medical directives or the local legal aid society may be hosting a free legal aid workshop for the community.

If you see something like this listed you should call the organizers and volunteer your services. Even if it is only for a few hours you can do a lot to help those who may be in need and it helps spread your name throughout the community. Be sure and take plenty of business cards to one of these events.

Chapter 16

Mobile Notary and Notary Signing Agent

You can make money as a normal in-home or office notary where people come to you. There is real money to make in the mobile notary and notary signing agent business.

Mobile Notary

A mobile notary is a notary public who travels to the client. This is especially helpful for business clients and people who are homebound, incarcerated or hospitalized.

Fees

A mobile notary is still bound by the maximum allowed fees as set-out in section 406 of the Government Code for notary services.

However, in addition to notary fees you can charge fees for travel, parking, tolls, waiting time, etc...

For instance you might have a minimum travel fee of $30.00 and increase it incrementally for each mile past the second mile from your home or office. You may charge a flat travel fee of $50.00 to the local hospital or jail.

For example, let's say you charge a flat travel fee of $50.00 to the local hospital. Now let's say you get a call requesting mobile notary services. You tell the caller up front that you charge $50.00 plus any applicable notary fees and that you charge $15.00 for each 15 minutes of waiting time after 30 minutes. You get to the hospital and wait 45 minutes to notarize an acknowledgment with one signature.

Here is how the fees would break down:

Travel Fee	$50.00
Waiting Fee	$15.00
Notary Fee	$6.00
Total Fee	$71.00

If you had performed this same service at home or in your office you would have only been able to charge $6.00.

Your fees should be reasonable and should be competitive with other mobile notary services in the area.

It may be a good idea to collect travel fees as soon as you arrive. That way if you must refuse to notarize the document, such as no identification being available for the signer, you will still have collected your travel fee.

Posting of Fees

A notary public in Texas must post their fees in their place of business. This is not really practical for a mobile notary. While your office may be in your home or in an office; your mobile notary clients will not be visiting you here.

My solution is to type a fee list, copy your sales tax permit and your commission and take them to an office supply store and have them reduce each copy to the size of ½ page and on one side have your commission and sales tax permit and on the other have your fee schedule and maybe a note explaining you are not an attorney and sample acknowledgment and jurat language. Then have this sheet laminated in thick plastic. This can then be shown to all of your mobile notary clients.

Receipts

You must make sure to provide an itemized receipt for mobile notary services. You must differentiate between notary fees and non-notary fees. Failure to leave a receipt or to itemize may make it appear as if you charged more than the statutory maximum for notary services.

You should also record the fee breakdown in your journal and document if the client refused a receipt.

Notary Signing Agent

A notary signing agent is a notary with more specialized education who notarizes mortgages and refinances.

As a notary signing agent you would be contacted by a lender, title company or signing service and be contracted out to do signings.

A notary signing agent should expect to make about $70.00 to $120.00 per assignment or even more depending on the type of loan and your experience, distance of travel, etc...

Often times you will need a laser printer and fax machine as most companies will send you the documents that need to be signed then you take them to the client. You will then need to send the documents back to the lender.

Signing agent work is fairly specialized and you should take a signing agent educational course before marketing yourself as a signing agent.

You will also need a background check which you can get from many places online. Beware of the fees though. Some places will charge you MUCH more than you need to pay for a background check. You may even be able to get one from your local police department or sheriff's office.

Chapter 17

Taxes and Accounting

One important aspect to running any business is keeping up with taxes and accounting. I am not a tax or accounting professional so my advice here will be limited. You should speak with an accountant or other professional with any specific questions.

Accounting

At a minimum I recommend using tax software and categorizing all income and expenditures. If you are going to open a business account use something like QuickBooks. If you will be operating your business with your personal checking account then Quicken Home and Business is a good product.

In addition to keeping track of income and expenses these programs will allow you to create professional invoices that you can send to your clients and should allow you to print end of the year statements that you can send out for people to give to tax preparers or accountants.

QuickBooks has a great payroll add-in that you can purchase. This makes it easy to run your own payroll.

Taxes

The last thing you want to do is get behind on taxes of any sort. It may be good to consult an accountant or at least do some thorough research to make sure you are filing and paying in a timely manner.

Income and Self Employment Tax

Your notary and non-notary income will be subject to federal income tax and you may be required to file estimated tax payments every quarter. Accounting software is very important and keeping track of income for these purposes.

Your non-notary fees will also be subject to self-employment tax. Notary fees are not subject to self-employment tax so you should make sure you document these in manner that separates them on your tax reports in the accounting software.

Sales Tax

You will need to keep track of your gross sales, sales subject to sales tax and the amount of sales tax you collected. You will receive a form the Texas Comptroller of Public Accounts every quarter to complete and you will send in any sales taxes you collected in the applicable time frame with the form.

Franchise Tax

Depending on your business structure you may be subject to a franchise tax. If this applies to you then you will receive a form every quarter to file with the Texas Comptroller of Public Accounts.

Chapter 18

Closing Shop

Unfortunately there will come a time when you may decide to close your notary business. This may mean not renewing or surrendering your notary commission or just mean that you will no longer be running a business but retain your notary commission. Either way you will need to know what to do and how to ensure you close your business in such a way that you cease your tax and other filing requirements.

Essentially you will need to identify each office that you contacted to obtain a permit, account or license and contact them to terminate your permit, account or license.

Surrender or Non-Renewal of Notary Commission

There are steps you need to take in the event you decide to either surrender or not renew your notary commission.

In either of these situations you must take all notarial records, including your journal and any documents you may have copy certified, and give them to your County Clerk. After depositing your records with the County Clerk you should receive a receipt.

It is important to deposit your records because this is where someone will go to get copies of any of your records or to browse the journals to look for an entry.

Remember; your records and journal help verify the legitimacy of a document that has your seal on it. If you are no longer commissioned as a notary public people can no longer come to you to verify the notarization of a document.

Surrender of Notary Commission

If you decide to surrender your notary commission you must send your current commission and a letter indicating your intent to voluntarily surrender your commission to the Secretary of State. For more information contact the Office of the Secretary of State.

You may write the Secretary of State at:

Notary Public Unit
PO Box 13375
Austin, TX 78711-3375

Closing Tax Accounts

If you close your business you should close all related tax accounts with each respective tax agency.

Sales and Franchise Tax Accounts

Your Sales and Use Tax Return will have a section to indicate the closure date of your business.

If you are subject to Franchise Tax there may be additional forms to complete to close your account.

IRS Account

If you obtained an EIN and you have decided to close your business you should write to the IRS to close your business account. After successfully closing your account will end the requirement that the business continue to file tax reports.

You cannot cancel your EIN. The EIN you have been issued will be permanently assigned to your business.

Surrendering Assumed Name

After closing your business you will need to contact your County Clerk's office to surrender your assumed name.

Closing Your Corporation or Partnership

To close your corporation or partnership you will need to contact the Secretary of State's office to get specific instructions and forms.

Death

In the event of your death a family member or the executor of your will should perform all of the steps outlined in this chapter. Your notary records will need to be turned over and all of your financial accounts closed.

Chapter 19

Frequently Asked Questions

The following FAQ's are taken from the Secretary of State's website. For more information or to read these FAQ's online please go to the following website: http://www.sos.state.tx.us/statdoc/faqs2300.shtml.

Who is eligible to become a notary public?

To be commissioned as a notary public in Texas, you must be a Texas resident at least 18 years of age who has not received a final conviction for a crime involving moral turpitude or a felony.

How do I become a notary public?

If you meet the eligibility requirements, submit the following to the secretary of state:

1. Completed Form 2301 (available from the secretary of state, county clerk, or your insurance agency or surety company);
2. Proof of a $10,000 surety bond; and
3. Filing fee of $21.

Once you are commissioned, you may purchase your required notary seal and record book from any office supply company.

How do I renew my notary public commission?

To renew your commission, submit the following to the secretary of state no earlier than 90 days before the expiration of your commission:

- Completed Form 2301 (available from the secretary of state, county clerk, or your insurance agency or surety company);
- Proof of a $10,000 surety bond; and
- Filing fee of $21.

May I change my name from the name shown on my Notary Public Commission?

Yes. A notary public may change the name on his or her commission by sending the secretary of state a name change application (Form 2305), his or her certificate of commission, a rider or endorsement from the insurance agency or surety showing the name change, and a $20 filing fee.

Do I need to keep a record book? What information should be included?

Yes. A Texas notary public is required to maintain a record book. This record book must be maintained whether or not any fees are charged for your notary public service. The following information must be included in the record book:

- the date of each instrument notarized;
- the date of the notarization;
- the name of the signer, grantor, or maker;
- the signer's, grantor's, or maker's residence or alleged residence;
- whether the signer, grantor, or maker is personally known by the notary public, was identified by an identification card issued by a United States federal or state governmental agency or a passport issued by the United States, or was introduced to the notary public and, if introduced, the name and residence or alleged residence of the individual introducing the signer, grantor, or maker;
- if the instrument is proved by a witness, the residence of the witness, whether the witness is personally known by the notary public or was introduced to the notary public and, if

introduced, the name and residence of the individual introducing the witness;

- the name and residence of the grantee;
- if land is conveyed or charged by the instrument, the name of the original grantee and the county where the land is located; and
- a brief description of the instrument.

Tex. Gov't Code §406.014

The person for whom a notarization is performed is not required to sign the record book.

A notary should not record any identification number that was assigned by a governmental agency or by the United States to the signer, grantor or maker on an identification card, driver's license, social security card or passport; or any other number that could be used to identify the signer, grantor or maker of the document. 1 Tex. Admin. Code §87.40. However, a notary is not prohibited from recording a number related to the residence or alleged residence of the signer, grantor or maker of the document or the instrument.

Can I get a copy of a notary's record book?

Yes. The entries in a notary's record book are public information and a notary is required to provide a certified copy of the record book to any person who requests, and pays the fees for, the copies. Tex. Gov't Code §406.014(b), (c). Although not required, the secretary of state suggests that you make all requests in writing, by sending a certified letter to the notary's official address on file with this Office. Making your request in this manner provides evidence of the request. Should a notary fail to respond or provide copies, you may file a complaint with this Office and include the evidence of the request as supporting documentation.

I am changing jobs and my current employer will not let me take my notary book, seal or commission with me. What should I do?

The employer is not the owner of a notary's record book or seal, even if the employer paid for the materials. Tex. Atty. Gen. Op. GA-0723. A Texas notary public is required by law to maintain a record book containing information on every notarization performed and is required to authenticate every official act with the seal of office. The record book is public information and a notary is required to produce copies of the book upon request. Therefore, the book and seal should remain in the possession of the notary at all times.

Similarly the secretary of state issues a commission to the individual notary public for a four-year term, without regard to who paid the application or bond fees. As a result, an employer may not retain the commission of an employee.

If your employer retains your seal, record book or commission when you leave your job, you should provide your employer a copy of Texas Attorney General Opinion GA-0723. If after receiving a copy of the opinion, your employer still will not let you take your notary book or seal with you, you should make a copy of the pages of the record book so that you can produce them upon request. You should also obtain a new seal and start a new record book for future notarizations. If your employer will not release your commission, you may contact the secretary of state's office for a duplicate copy of the commission.

Is a notary public seal required?

Yes. A notary public shall provide a seal of office that clearly shows, when embossed, stamped, or printed on a document, the words "Notary Public, State of Texas" around a star of five points, the notary public's name, and the date the notary public's commission expires. The notary public shall authenticate all official acts with the seal of office.

How long should I keep my record book?

A notary is required to keep, in a safe and secure manner, copies of the records of notarizations performed for the longer of: 1) the term of the commission in which the notarization occurred; or 2) three years following the date of notarization. 1 Tex. Admin. Code §87.44. The best practice, however, would be for the notary to permanently maintain copies of the records.

What do I do with my stamp/seal when my commission expires or I am no longer a notary public

When the commission of a notary public expires, or the individual otherwise ceases to be a notary public, the notary seal should be destroyed to prevent possible misuse by another individual.

May I notarize my spouse's signature? May I notarize for my spouse's business? May I notarize for my relatives?

There is no specific prohibition against notarizing a spouse's or relative's signature or notarizing for a spouse's business. However, notarizations should not be performed by a notary public who is a party to the instrument or financially or beneficially interested in the transaction. The facts in each situation will determine whether the notary's action was proper.

Can a notary notarize a document in which his or her employer has an interest?

Yes. In fact, there are statutes that specifically permit such notarizations. For example, §121.002 of the Texas Civil Practice and Remedies Code authorizes an employee of a corporation to take an acknowledgment of a written instrument in which the corporation has an interest. In addition, §199.002 of the Texas Finance Code specifies that a notary public is not disqualified from performing a notarization of a document, solely because of the notary public's ownership of stock or participation in or employment by a state trust company that has an interest in the underlying transaction.

Is a government employee required to notarize documents for the general public?

No. The Texas Attorney General's office issued a letter opinion in 1988 indicating that a notary public who is employed by a governmental body may refuse to take acknowledgements for the general public and must refuse when doing so would interfere with the employee's discharge of his or her duties as a public employee. Tex. Atty. Gen. Op. LO-88-34.

May I make a certified copy of a birth certificate or a marriage license?

No. Birth certificates and marriage licenses are publically recordable documents. Recordable documents are recorded with some specific governmental entity, such as the secretary of state's office, a court of law, a county clerk, or the Bureau of Vital Statistics. A certified copy of a recordable document may be obtained by contacting the recording entity. A notary cannot make certified copies of recordable documents.

A notary may, however, make a certified copy of a non-recordable document. A non-recordable document is one that cannot be recorded with any type of governmental entity. For instance, a letter is not recorded with anyone, but there are times the sender of the letter would like to maintain a certified copy of that letter for his or her file.

May I take an acknowledgement over the telephone?

No. The person for whom a notarization is performed must personally appear before the notary public at the time the notarization is performed.

May I perform notarial acts in all counties in Texas?

Yes. A notary public has statewide jurisdiction and may perform notarial acts in any county in the state of Texas.

May a notary public determine which type of notarial certificate should be attached to a document?

No. A notary public who is not an attorney should only complete a notarial certificate which is already on the document, or type or attach a certificate of the maker's choosing. If a notary public were presented with a document that did not contain a certificate and decided which certificate to attach, that notary public would be "practicing law." Instead, the notary may allow the person for whom the notarization is performed to choose among the sample certificates provided to the notary with the notary's commission.

May I advertise in a language other than English?

Yes, but you must include notice containing the following statement with the advertisement:

> "I AM NOT AN ATTORNEY LICENSED TO PRACTICE LAW IN TEXAS AND MAY NOT GIVE LEGAL ADVICE OR ACCEPT FEES FOR LEGAL ADVICE."

In addition to containing the above statement, the notice must be conspicuous, be in both English and the language of the advertisement, and must include the fees that a notary public may charge.

Use of the phrase "notario publico" is prohibited.

How much does it cost to get a document notarized?

Texas Government Code §406.024 specifies the maximum fees for an official act performed by a notary public. A lesser fee is allowed or no fee at all may be charged. Excessive fees are grounds for disciplinary action.

Does the employer or the notary determine the fee charged for notary services performed during the employer's office hours?

Texas Government Code §406.024 specifies that the notary public or the notary's employer may charge the specified fees.

How do I obtain an apostille/certificate on my school transcript or diploma?

Follow one of these two options for school documents:

- Notarization of ORIGINAL school records would require you to return to the school to have the school official sign an affidavit in the presence of the notary public.
- For notarization of a PHOTOCOPY of the original school record, the owner of the original document must sign an affidavit on the photocopy, in the presence of the notary public. In either case, the notary must complete the appropriate notarial certificate acknowledging the date the signer appeared before him/her.

A notary public can make a certified copy of a diploma but NOT other school documents.

After obtaining the notarized documents, follow the instructions stated in the answer to the question below.

How do I obtain an official certificate or apostille on a notarization?

You may obtain an official certificate or apostille on a document notarized by a Texas notary public from the Authentications Unit of the secretary of state. Detailed information pertaining to the procedure for requesting certificates or apostilles may be found on our web site.

The Texas Secretary of State cannot provide certification for notaries commissioned outside the state of Texas.

What do I do if I lose my seal or notary book?

Every commissioned notary public has a duty to safeguard his/her notary materials. However, if your notary seal or record book has been misplaced or lost, send a letter to this office detailing the circumstances in which the materials went missing, the last time you used it, and any other relevant information. If any of your notary materials have been stolen, you should file a report with your local law enforcement office and enclose a copy of that report with your letter to this office. Send the letter to the Notary Public Unit, P.O. Box 13375, Austin, Texas 78711-3375 or by email.

Remember that you have a duty to record every notarial act in your record book. Therefore, if your notary record book is lost or stolen, you must get a new book before you resume providing notarial services. Similarly, you must get a new seal if your seal is lost or stolen, as notaries are required to affix their seals to all official acts they perform.

Are there restrictions on the way an instrument is signed?

A notary must sign the notarial certificate using the same name that is listed on the commission issued by the secretary of state. However, as long as the name matches, the signature of the notary may be printed, written, typed, stamped, etc.

The individual signing the document may sign in whatever manner he/she chooses. The name or manner of signing used by the signor is not the responsibility of the notary public. However, the notary public does have a responsibility to make sure that the information contained in the notarial certificate is accurate. For example if John Doe appears before a notary public and signs the instrument with an "X" the notary public should still state in the notarial certificate that John Doe personally appeared on a given date.

What are the requirements for performing an electronic notarization?

Any Texas notary may perform an electronic notarization. An electronic notarization must meet all of the requirements of any other notarization, such as the requirement that the signer personally appear before the notary to acknowledge the document. In addition, the notary's electronic seal must reproduce the required elements of the notary seal.

In addition, the Texas Uniform Electronic Transaction Act ("TUETA") applies to transactions that the parties agree to conduct electronically. TUETA includes a section providing for an electronic notarization:

§322.011. NOTARIZATION AND ACKNOWLEDGMENT. If a law requires a signature or record to be notarized, acknowledged, verified, or made under oath, the requirement is satisfied if the electronic signature of the person authorized to perform those acts, together with all other information required to be included by other applicable law, is attached to or logically associated with the signature or record.

Can I complete a Form I-9, Employment Eligibility Verification, on behalf of an employer?

No. Although the United States Citizenship and Immigration Services (USCIS) would allow a notary public to fill out Form I-9 on the behalf of an employer, Texas notaries public are not provided this authority under Texas law. Therefore, if an employer requests that you complete any portion of a Form I-9 in your capacity as a notary public, you should refuse.

Can a private employer restrict the notarial activities of an employee during work hours?

Yes. The Texas Attorney General's office has issued an opinion supporting the authority of a private employer to limit or prohibit the notarial activities of its employees during work hours. Tex. Atty. Gen. Op. GA-0723.

Does a Texas notary public have jurisdiction on a U.S. military base or Indian reservation?

Maybe not. Texas notaries have statewide jurisdiction. Gov't Code § 406.003. Accordingly, a Texas notary does not appear to be authorized to take an oath or acknowledgement, or perforapter m any other notarial act, on a federal enclave or an Indian reservation. See Tex. Atty. Gen. Op. JC-0390 (2001) (finding that engineers practicing on a federal enclave are not required to be licensed in Texas). Some, but not all military bases are federal enclaves. To find out if a particular military base is a federal enclave, start your search by emailing us to find out if we have record of a deed of cession. If we do not have a deed of cession, it does not necessarily mean it does not exist. You should consult your private attorney to determine whether the property in question was ceded

Chapter 20

Applicable Laws and Regulations

This section contains copies of the applicable laws and regulations pertaining to the office of notary public. Please note that these laws and regulations are subject to legislative change and are current as of the date of publication of this book.

Section 406 Texas Government Code

Sec. 406.001. APPOINTMENTS

The secretary of state may appoint a notary public at any time.

Sec. 406.002. TERM

The term of a notary public expires four years after the date the notary public qualifies.

Sec. 406.003. JURISDICTION

A notary public has statewide jurisdiction.

Sec. 406.004. ELIGIBILITY

Each person appointed and commissioned as a notary public shall be at least 18 years of age and a resident of the State of Texas and must not have been convicted of a felony or crime involving moral turpitude.

Sec. 406.005. APPOINTMENT PROCEDURE—STATEMENT

(a) Each person to be appointed a notary public shall submit an application to the secretary of state on a form prescribed by the secretary of state. The application must satisfy the secretary of state that the applicant is qualified. The application must state:

(1) the applicant's name to be used in acting as a notary public;

(2) the applicant's post office address;

(3) the applicant's county of residence;

(4) the applicant's date of birth;

(5) the applicant's driver's license number or the number of other official state-issued identification; and

(6) the applicant's social security number.

(b) The applicant shall also execute the statement of officers as required by Section 1, Article XVI, Texas Constitution.

Sec. 406.006. QUALIFICATION

An individual qualifies by:

(1) properly completing the application form;

(2) executing the statement;

(3) providing the bond, if required;

(4) paying the required filing fees; and

(5) meeting the eligibility requirements.

Sec. 406.007. FEES PAID TO SECRETARY OF STATE

(a) The applicant must submit to the secretary of state:

(1) a fee of $10 for approving and filing the bond of the notary public, if required; and

(2) a fee of $1 to be appropriated to and used by the secretary of state only for hiring an investigator and for preparing and distributing the materials required to be distributed under Section 406.008.

(b) The secretary of state shall charge for use of the state a fee of $10 for a notary public commission. The applicant must pay the fee in advance to the secretary of state.

Sec. 406.008. COMMISSION; NOTARY MATERIALS

(a) Immediately after the qualification of a notary public, the secretary of state shall send notice of appointment along with a commission to the notary public. The commission is effective as of the date of qualification.

(b) When the commission is issued, the secretary of state shall supply the notary public with:

(1) materials outlining the powers and duties of the office;

(2) a list of prohibited acts; and

(3) sample forms for an acknowledgment, jurat, and verification and for the administering of an oath, protest, and deposition.

Sec. 406.009. REJECTION OF APPOINTMENT; SUSPENSION OR REVOCATION OF COMMISSION

(a) The secretary of state may, for good cause, reject an application or suspend or revoke the commission of a notary public.

(b) An action by the secretary of state under this section is subject to the rights of notice, hearing, adjudication, and appeal.

(c) An appeal under this section is to the district court of Travis County. The secretary of state has the burden of proof, and the trial is conducted de novo.

(d) In this section, "good cause" includes:

(1) a final conviction for a crime involving moral turpitude;

(2) a false statement knowingly made in an application;

(3) the failure to comply with Section 406.017;

(4) a final conviction for a violation of a law concerning the regulation of the conduct of notaries public in this or another state;

(5) the imposition on the notary public of an administrative, criminal, or civil penalty for a violation

of a law or rule prescribing the duties of a notary public; or

(6) performing any notarization when the person for whom the notarization is performed did not personally appear before the notary at the time the notarization is executed.

(e) The following may not be considered a conviction for the purposes of determining eligibility and good cause:

(1) a dismissal of a proceeding against the defendant and discharge of the defendant before an adjudication of guilt; and

(2) a finding of guilt that has been set aside.

Sec. 406.010. BOND; OATH

(a) Each person to be appointed a notary public shall, before entering the official duties of office, execute a bond in the amount of $10,000 with a solvent surety company authorized to do business in this state as a surety. The bond must be approved by the secretary of state, payable to the governor, and conditioned on the faithful performance of the duties of office. The secretary of state has the authority to accept an electronic filing of the notary public bond if an agreement has been made with the surety company.

(b) The notary bond shall be deposited in the office of the secretary of state, is not void on first recovery, and may be sued on in the name of the injured party from time to time until the whole amount of the bond is recovered.

(c) A notary public, before entering on the duties of office, shall take the official oath required by Section 1, Article XVI, Texas Constitution.

(d) The oath shall be signed and sworn to or affirmed by the notary public in the presence of a notary public or other person authorized to administer oaths in this state. A notary public cannot execute his or her own oath of office.

(e) The secretary of state shall provide an oath of office form along with the commission and educational materials.

(f) Subsections (a) and (b) do not apply to a person whose services as a notary public are performed primarily as a state officer or employee.

Sec. 406.011. REAPPOINTMENT

(a) Not earlier than 90 days prior to the expiration date of the notary's term, a notary public may apply for reappointment on submission of a new application to the secretary of state.

(b) A notary public who is not reappointed on or before the expiration date of the term the notary public is serving will be appointed for a new term expiring four years from the date of qualification.

Sec. 406.012. INSPECTION OF RECORDS

All records concerning the appointment and qualification of the notary public shall be kept in the office of the secretary of state. The records are public information.

Sec. 406.013. SEAL

(a) A notary public shall provide a seal of office that clearly shows, when embossed, stamped, or printed on a document, the words "Notary Public, State of Texas" around a star of five points, the notary public's name, and the date the notary public's commission expires. The notary public shall authenticate all official acts with the seal of office.

(b) The seal may be a circular form not more than two inches in diameter or a rectangular form not more than one inch in width and 2-1/2 inches in length. The seal must have a serrated or milled edge border.

(c) The seal must be affixed by a seal press or stamp that embosses or prints a seal that legibly reproduces the required elements of the seal under photographic methods. An indelible ink pad must be used for affixing by a stamp the impression of a seal on an instrument to authenticate the notary public's official act.

(d) Subsection (c) does not apply to an electronically transmitted authenticated document, except that an electronically transmitted authenticated document must legibly reproduce the required elements of the seal.

Sec. 406.014. NOTARY RECORDS

(a) A notary public other than a court clerk notarizing instruments for the court shall keep in a book a record of:

(1) the date of each instrument notarized;

(2) the date of the notarization;

(3) the name of the signer, grantor, or maker;

(4) the signer's, grantor's, or maker's residence or alleged residence;

(5) whether the signer, grantor, or maker is personally known by the notary public, was identified by an identification card issued by a governmental agency or a passport issued by the United States, or was introduced to the notary public and, if introduced, the name and residence or alleged residence of the individual introducing the signer, grantor, or maker;

(6) if the instrument is proved by a witness, the residence of the witness, whether the witness is personally known by the notary public or was introduced to the notary public and, if introduced, the name and residence of the individual introducing the witness;

(7) the name and residence of the grantee;

(8) if land is conveyed or charged by the instrument, the name of the original grantee and the county where the land is located; and

(9) a brief description of the instrument.

(b) Entries in the notary's book are public information.

(c) A notary public shall, on payment of all fees, provide a certified copy of any record in the notary public's office to any person requesting the copy.

(d) A notary public who administers an oath pursuant to Article 45.019, Code of Criminal Procedure, is exempt from the requirement in Subsection (a) of recording that oath.

(e) A notary public may maintain the records required by Subsection (a) electronically in a computer or other storage device.

Sec. 406.015. COPIES CERTIFIED BY COUNTY CLERK

(a) A copy of a record, declaration, protest, or other official act of a notary public may be certified by the county clerk with whom the instrument is deposited.

(b) A copy of an instrument certified by the county clerk under Subsection (a) has the same authority as if certified by the notary public by whom the record, declaration, protest, or other official act was originally made.

Sec. 406.016. AUTHORITY

(a) A notary public has the same authority as the county clerk to:

(1) take acknowledgments or proofs of written instruments;

(2) protest instruments permitted by law to be protested;

(3) administer oaths;

(4) take depositions; and

(5) certify copies of documents not recordable in the public records.

(b) A notary public shall sign an instrument in Subsection (a) in the name under which the notary public is commissioned.

(c) A notary public may not issue an identification card.

(d) A notary public not licensed to practice law in this state may not give legal advice or accept fees for legal advice.

Sec. 406.0165. SIGNING DOCUMENT FOR INDIVIDUAL WITH DISABILITY

(a) A notary may sign the name of an individual who is physically unable to sign or make a mark on a document presented for notarization if directed to do so by that individual, in the presence of a witness who has no legal or equitable interest in any real or personal property that is the subject of, or is affected by, the document being signed. The notary shall require identification of the witness in the same manner as from an acknowledging person under Section 121.005, Civil Practice and Remedies Code.

(a) A notary who signs a document under this section shall write, beneath the signature, the following or a substantially similar sentence:

(b) "Signature affixed by notary in the presence of (name of witness), a disinterested witness, under Section 406.0165, Government Code."

(c) A signature made under this section is effective as the signature of the individual on whose behalf the signature was made for any purpose. A subsequent bona fide purchaser for value may rely on the signature of the notary as evidence of the individual's consent to execution of the document.

(d) In this section, "disability" means a physical impairment that impedes the ability to sign or make a mark on a document.

Sec. 406.017. REPRESENTATION AS ATTORNEY

(a) A person commits an offense if the person is a notary public and the person:

(1) states or implies that the person is an attorney licensed to practice law in this state;

(2) solicits or accepts compensation to prepare documents for or otherwise represent the interest of another in a judicial or administrative proceeding, including a proceeding relating to immigration to the United States, United States citizenship, or related matters;

(3) solicits or accepts compensation to obtain relief of any kind on behalf of another from any officer, agency, or employee of this state or the United States;

(4) uses the phrase "notario" or "notario publico" to advertise the services of a notary public, whether by signs, pamphlets, stationery, or other written communication or by radio or television; or

(5) advertises the services of a notary public in a language other than English, whether by signs, pamphlets, stationery, or other written communication or by radio or television, if the person does not post or otherwise include with the advertisement a notice that complies with Subsection (b).

(b) The notice required by Subsection (a)(5) must state that the notary public is not an attorney and must be in English and in the language of the advertisement and in letters of a conspicuous size. If the advertisement is by radio or television, the statement may be modified, but must include substantially the same message. The notice must include the fees that a notary public may charge and the following statement:

(c) "I AM NOT AN ATTORNEY LICENSED TO PRACTICE LAW IN TEXAS AND MAY NOT GIVE LEGAL ADVICE OR ACCEPT FEES FOR LEGAL ADVICE."

(d) It is an exception to prosecution under this section that, at the time of the conduct charged, the person is licensed to practice law in this state and in good standing with the State Bar of Texas.

(e) Except as provided by Subsection (e) of this section, an offense under this section is a Class A misdemeanor.

(f) An offense under this section is a felony of the third degree if it is shown on the trial of the offense that the defendant has previously been convicted under this section.

(g) Failure to comply with this section is, in addition to a violation of any other applicable law of this state, a deceptive trade practice actionable under Chapter 17, Business & Commerce Code.

Sec. 406.018. REMOVAL FROM OFFICE

(a) A notary public guilty of wilful neglect of duty or malfeasance in office may be removed from office in the manner provided by law.

(b) A notary public indicted for and convicted of a wilful neglect of duty or official misconduct shall be removed from office. The court shall include the order for removal as part of its judgment.

Sec. 406.019. CHANGE OF ADDRESS

A notary public shall notify the secretary of state of a change of the notary public's address not later than the 10th day after the date on which the change is made.

Sec. 406.020. REMOVAL FROM STATE

A notary public who removes his residence from this state vacates the office.

Sec. 406.021. REMOVAL FROM PRECINCT

An ex officio notary public who moves permanently from the notary public's precinct vacates the office.

Sec. 406.022. EFFECT OF VACANCY

If the office of a notary public becomes vacant due to resignation, removal, or death, the county clerk of the county in which the notary public resides shall obtain the record books and public papers belonging to the office of the notary public and deposit them in the county clerk's office.

Sec. 406.023. ADMINISTRATION AND ENFORCEMENT

(a) The secretary of state shall adopt rules necessary for the administration and enforcement of this subchapter. The rules must be consistent with the provisions of this subchapter.

(b) The secretary of state may employ an investigator to aid in the enforcement of this subchapter.

(c) The secretary of state may provide for the appointment of county clerks as deputy custodians for the limited authentication of notary public records deposited in the clerks' offices.

Sec. 406.024. FEES CHARGED BY NOTARY PUBLIC

(a) A notary public or its employer may charge the following fees:

   (1) for protesting a bill or note for non-acceptance or nonpayment, register and seal, a fee of $4;

   (2) for each notice of protest, a fee of $1;

   (3) for protesting in all other cases, a fee of $4;

   (4) for certificate and seal to a protest, a fee of $4;

(5) for taking the acknowledgment or proof of a deed or other instrument in writing, for registration, including certificate and seal, a fee of $6 for the first signature and $1 for each additional signature;
(6) for administering an oath or affirmation with certificate and seal, a fee of $6;
(7) for a certificate under seal not otherwise provided for, a fee of $6;
(8) for a copy of a record or paper in the notary public's office, a fee of 50 cents for each page;
(9) for taking the deposition of a witness, 50 cents for each 100 words;
(10)for swearing a witness to a deposition, certificate, seal, and other business connected with taking the deposition, a fee of $6; and
(11)for a notarial act not provided for, a fee of $6.

(b) A notary public may charge a fee only for an acknowledgment or official act under Subsection (a). The fee charged may not exceed the fee authorized by Subsection (a).

Sec. 406.025. SIGNATURE ON COMMISSIONS AFTER CHANGE IN OFFICE

If the governor or secretary of state ceases to hold or perform the duties of office, existing stocks of commissions bearing the person's printed name, signature, or facsimile signature may be used until they are exhausted, and the person succeeding to the office or the duties of the office shall have the commissions issued with:

(1) the obsolete printed name, signature, or facsimile signature struck through;
(2) the successor's printed name submitted for the obsolete printed name, signature, or facsimile signature; and
(3) the inscription "Printed name authorized by law" near the successor's printed name.

Title 1 Texas Administrative Code, Chapter 87

§87.1 Application for Commission as a Notary Public

(a) The secretary of state appoints notaries public under the provisions of article IV, §26 of the Texas Constitution and Chapter 406, Government Code.

(b) All persons applying for a notary public commission shall use the application form prescribed by the secretary of state.

(c) The application form is available on the secretary of state web site at www.sos.state.tx.us/statdoc/statforms.shtml or may be obtained by writing the Office of the Secretary of State, Notary Public Unit, P.O. Box 13375, Austin, Texas 78711. See form 2301. The application form for a notary who is an officer or employee of a state agency is form 2301-NB, available on the web site of the State Office of Risk Management at www.sorm.state.tx.us.

§87.2 Eligibility to Hold the Office of Notary Public

(a) Subject to the provision in subsection (b) of this section and §87.70 of this title (relating to Qualification by an Escrow Officer Residing in an Adjacent State), a person is eligible to be a notary public if the person is 18 years of age or older and a resident of Texas.

(b) A person is not eligible to be a notary public if the person was convicted of a crime involving moral turpitude or a felony and the conviction has become final, has not been set aside, and no pardon or certificate of restoration of citizenship rights has been granted.

(c) If an applicant is not eligible, the secretary of state will reject the application.

(d) If the secretary of state discovers, at any time, that an applicant or commissioned notary public is not eligible, the secretary of state will reject the notary application or revoke the notary commission.

§87.3 Issuance of the Notary Public Commission by the Secretary of State

(a) The secretary of state shall commission a qualified applicant. An applicant is qualified if:
   (1) the applicant meets the eligibility requirements stated in §87.2 of this title (relating to Eligibility to Hold the Office of Notary Public);
   (2) the applicant submits:
      (A) a properly completed and executed application;
      (B) the bond as provided in §406.010, Government Code, if required;
      (C) the statement of officer and oath of office required by article XVI, §1 Texas Constitution;
      (D) payment to the secretary of state of fees required by §406.007, Government Code; and
   (3) no good cause exists for rejecting the application.

(b) The secretary of state shall not commission an applicant if the applicant had a prior application rejected or a commission revoked for a finding of ineligibility or good cause and the reason for ineligibility or grounds for good cause continues to exist.

(c) When all conditions for qualification have been met, the application shall be approved, stamped "qualified" with the date of qualification, and filed. The secretary of state shall cause a commission to be issued and sent to each notary public who has qualified. A commission is effective as of the date of qualification.

(d) If an application is not properly completed and executed, the qualification of the applicant will be delayed. The secretary of state shall notify the applicant in writing stating the reason or reasons why the commission was not issued, and the steps which must be taken to correct the errors or omissions. The applicant shall have 30 days from the date of the notice to respond; otherwise, the application will be considered abandoned and all fees deposited forfeited.

§87.4 Qualification by an Officer or Employee of a State Agency Who Does Not Furnish a Notary Public Bond

(a) An applicant who is an officer or employee of a state agency is not required to provide a surety bond. For the purpose of this chapter, "state agency" has the meaning assigned by §2052.101, Government Code.

(b) An applicant who is an officer or employee of a state agency and does not provide a surety bond must complete the notary public application entitled "Application for Appointment as a Notary Public Without Bond" (Form 2301-NB).

(c) The State Agency employing the applicant must submit the completed application to the State Office of Risk Management.

(d) The State Office of Risk Management shall complete the verification certificate on the application and forward the completed application to the Office of the Secretary of State for processing.

(e) The secretary of state shall commission the applicant if:

  (1) the applicant meets the eligibility requirements stated in §87.2 of this title (relating to Eligibility to Hold the Office of Notary Public);

  (2) the applicant submits:

    (A) a properly completed and executed application verified by the State Office of Risk Management;

(B) the statement of officer and oath of office required by article XVI, §1 Texas Constitution;

(C) the payment of fees required by §406.007(a)(2) and §406.007(b), Government Code; and

(3) no good cause exists for rejecting the application.

§87.5 Change in Employment Status by an Officer or Employee of a State Agency Who Has Qualified Without a Surety Bond

(a) If a notary public who has qualified without a surety bond transfers to another state agency, the agency to which the notary public transfers shall notify the State Office of Risk Management and the Office of the Secretary of State of the transfer.

(b) If a notary public terminates state employment, the notary public shall:

(1) voluntarily surrender the notary public commission;

(2) purchase and provide evidence to the secretary of state of the purchase of a notary public bond for the time period remaining on the notary's current term of office; or

(3) apply for a new term of office, provide a notary public bond, and pay the applicable fees.

(c) Failure to take one of the actions set forth in subsection (b) of this section within 30 days of termination of state employment is good cause for revocation of the notary public's commission.

§87.6 Renewal of Commission

(a) A notary may renew the commission by filing an application for renewal in the same manner and on the same form as if the notary was filing an original application for commission. The secretary of state will accept applications for renewal not sooner than 90 days before the expiration of the notary public's current commission. The renewal must be received by the secretary of state no later than the expiration date of the notary public's current commission.

(b) The secretary of state shall determine eligibility for renewals according to the same standards as initial applicants, in accordance with §87.2 of this title (relating to Eligibility to Hold the Office of Notary Public) and §406.004, Government Code. The secretary of state is not bound by prior determinations of eligibility.

§87.10 Rejection of Application and Revocation of Commission

The secretary of state shall, for ineligibility or good cause, reject any application, revoke the commission of any notary public, or take other disciplinary action, as outlined in §87.24 of this title (relating to Disciplinary Action), against a notary public as the secretary of state deems appropriate. Rejection, revocation, and disciplinary proceedings will be held pursuant to the right of notice, hearing, and adjudication as set out in the rules of practice and procedure before the Office of the Secretary of State, the rules of the State Office of Administrative Hearings and the Administrative Procedure Act, Government Code, §§2001.001 - 2001.902. Any party to a contested case has the right to be represented by legal counsel. Such action will be subject to the right of appeal to a district court of Travis County.

§87.11 Good Cause

(a) Good cause may include the following:

(1) ineligibility due to a final felony conviction;

(2) ineligibility due to a final conviction for a crime involving moral turpitude;

(3) a false statement knowingly made in a notary public application;

(4) a final conviction for the violation of any law concerning the regulation of the conduct of notaries public in this state or any other state;
(5) use of the phrase "notario" or "notario publico" in connection with advertising or offering the services of a notary public;
(6) false representation as an attorney as specified in §406.017, Government Code;
(7) a failure to fully and faithfully discharge any of the duties or responsibilities required of a notary public;
(8) the unauthorized practice of law;
(9) a failure to utilize a correct notary seal as described in §406.013, Government Code;
(10)a failure to administer an oath or affirmation as required by law;
(11)the collection of a fee in excess of the fees authorized by §406.024, Government Code;
(12)the execution of any certificate as a notary public containing a statement known to the notary public to be false;
(13)a failure to complete the notarial certificate at the time the notary public's signature and seal are affixed to the document;
(14)the advertising or holding out in any manner that the notary public is an immigration specialist, immigration consultant, or any other title or description reflecting an expertise in immigration matters;
(15)the use of false or misleading advertising of either an oral or written nature, whereby the notary public has represented or indicated that he or she has duties, rights, powers, or privileges that are not possessed by law;
(16)performing a notarization when the purported signer did not personally appear before the notary at the time the notarization is executed;

(17)previous disciplinary action against the notary public in accordance with these sections;

(18)a failure to comply with, or violation of, a previous disciplinary action taken pursuant to §87.24 of this title (relating to Disciplinary Action); and

(19)a failure to respond to a request for public information.

(b) A crime involving moral turpitude means the commission of a crime involving dishonesty, fraud, deceit, misrepresentation, deliberate violence, or that reflects adversely on the applicant's honesty, trustworthiness, or fitness as a notary public, which may include, but not be limited to:

(1) Class A and B type misdemeanors; and

(2) felony convictions which have not been set aside, or for which no pardon or certificate of restoration of citizenship rights have been granted.

(c) Final Class C type misdemeanor convictions shall not be considered in determining good cause.

§87.20 Qualification Under New Name

During the four-year term of office, a notary public may change the name on the notary commission by submitting the following to the secretary of state:

(1) an Application for Change of Name as a Texas Notary Public (Form 2305 available on the secretary of state web site at www.sos.state.tx.us/statdoc/statforms.shtml);

(2) a rider or endorsement to the bond on file with the secretary of state from the surety company or its agent or representative specifying the change of name;

(3) the current certificate of commission or a signed and notarized statement that the notary public will perform all future notarial acts under the name specified on the amended commission; and

(4) the statutory fees for the issuance of a commission and the filing of a bond.

§87.21 Rejection of Change of Name

If the submission of the change of name does not comply with §87.20 of this title (relating to Qualification Under New Name), the secretary of state shall notify the notary public in writing of any deficiency. The notary public shall have 30 days from the date of the notice to respond. If no response is received within that time period, the request for the change of name will be considered abandoned and all fees paid will be forfeited.

§87.22 Issuance of Amended Commission

If the submission of the change of name complies with §87.20 of this title (relating to Qualification Under New Name), the secretary of state shall issue an amended commission to the notary public in the name requested. Upon issuance of the amended commission, the notary public must perform all notarial acts using the name on the amended commission.

§87.23 complaint Procedures

(a) A person harmed by the actions of a notary public may file a complaint with the secretary of state. The complaint shall be filed on the form prescribed by the secretary of state for such purposes, shall be signed and verified by the person alleging misconduct on the part of the notary public, shall include copies of the notarized documents that are the subject of the complaint, and shall substantially comply with the requirements set forth on the prescribed form.

(b) The secretary of state may determine that the allegations in the complaint are not sufficient to warrant formal disciplinary action. In such case, the secretary of state may:

  (1) take no action on the complaint;

(2) informally advise the notary public of the appropriate conduct and the applicable statutes and rules governing the conduct; or

(3) request further information from the complainant or the notary prior to taking action.

(c) If the secretary of state determines that the complaint alleges sufficient facts to constitute good cause for disciplinary action against the notary public, the secretary of state shall send a copy of the complaint to the notary public with a request to the notary to respond to the statements in the complaint.

(d) The notary public must respond to the complaint in writing. The response must:

(1) specify any disputed facts and provide such additional information as the notary public shall desire;

(2) be signed and sworn to by the notary before a person authorized to administer oaths;

(3) include copies of the pages of the notary record book referencing the notarization that is the subject of the complaint; and

(4) be received by the secretary of state within 20 days of mailing of the copy of the complaint to the notary public.

(e) The secretary of state shall review the response and determine whether further administrative action is appropriate. If the secretary determines that no further action is appropriate, the secretary shall notify the notary public and the complainant of the determination in writing.

(f) If the secretary determines that further administrative action is appropriate, the secretary shall follow the procedures set forth in §87.24 of this title (relating to Disciplinary Action).

§87.24 Disciplinary Action

(a) The secretary of state has discretion to determine that the conduct that forms the basis of a complaint against a notary public does not warrant disciplinary action against the notary public and take no further action on the complaint. If the secretary of state determines that disciplinary action should be taken the secretary of state may pursue the following disciplinary actions:

  (1) an official reprimand to the notary public; or

  (2) an agreement by the notary to:

    (A) not engage in any further misconduct;

    (B) to voluntarily surrender the notary public commission;

    (C) to accept a suspension of the notary public commission for a set period of time;

    (D) to complete a course of study relating to the powers, duties, and responsibilities of a notary public;

    (E) not seek renewal of a notary public commission for a specified period of time; or

    (F) to take such other action as the secretary deems appropriate; or

  (3) revocation of the notary commission.

(b) If no agreement can be reached, before taking action to suspend or revoke the notary public commission, the secretary of state shall give written notice to the notary of a right to a hearing in accordance with the rules of practice and procedure before the secretary of state. If a hearing is timely requested, the secretary of state shall follow the provisions of the Administrative Procedure Act, Chapter 2001, Texas Government Code governing the initiation and conduct of a contested case proceeding.

(c) It is within the secretary of state's discretion to determine that no action should be taken or to enter into an agreement with the notary regarding the appropriate action. The secretary of state shall close the notary complaint file upon a determination that no further action is necessary or conclusion of an agreement with the notary. After the notary complaint file is closed, the secretary of state will take no further action on the complaint and will not accept an additional complaint with the same or substantially same allegations.

§87.25 Time for Action

The secretary of state may take disciplinary action for an act or omission which occurred during a prior term of office.

§87.30 Refusal of Requests for Notarial Services

(a) A notary is authorized to refuse to perform a notarial act if:

   (1) the notary has reasonable grounds to believe that the signer is acting under coercion or undue influence;

   (2) the notary has reasonable grounds to believe that the document in connection with which the notarial act is requested may be used for an unlawful or improper purpose;

   (3) the notary has concerns about the capacity of the signing party to understand the contents of the document;

   (4) the notary is not familiar with the type of notarization requested.

(b) A notary who is employed by a governmental body shall not perform notarial services that interfere with the notary's discharge of the notary's duties as a public employee.

(c) A notary may not refuse a request for notarial services on the basis of the sex, age, religion, race, ethnicity or national origin of the requesting party.

(d) A notary should refuse request for notarial services only after careful deliberation.

§87.40 Prohibition Against Recording Personal Information

(a) A notary public (other than a court clerk notarizing instruments for the court) shall not record in the notary's record book:

   (1) an identification number that was assigned by a governmental agency or by the United States to the signer, grantor or maker and that is set forth on the identification card or passport presented as identification; or

   (2) any other number that could be used to identify the signer, grantor or maker of the document.

(b) This section does not prohibit a notary from recording a number related to the residence of the signer, grantor or maker of the document or the instrument.

§87.41 Form of Record Book

A notary may maintain the notary record book electronically in a computer or other storage device so long as the records from that book are adequately backed-up and are capable of being printed in a tangible medium when requested.

§87.42 Public Information

Entries in the notary public record book are public information. On payment of all fees, the notary shall promptly provide a certified copy of any record in the notary public's record book to any person requesting the copy. If the notary has inadvertently included personal identifiable information in the record book contrary to §87.40 of this title (relating to Prohibition Against Recording Personal Information), the notary must redact that personal information prior to release of the information.

§87.43 Failure to Provide Public Information

Failure to respond to a request for public information may be good cause for suspension or revocation of a notary commission or other disciplinary action against the notary.

§87.44 Records Retention

A notary shall retain, in a safe and secure manner, copies of the records of notarization performed for the longer of the term of the commission in which the notarization occurred or three years following the date of notarization.

§87.50 Change of Address

(a) A notary must notify the secretary of state in writing of a change in address within 10 days of the change. To notify the secretary of state of a change of address, the notary should complete and submit form 2302 (Notary Public Change of Address Form). This form is available on the secretary of state web site at www.sos.state.tx.us/statdoc/statforms.shtml.

(b) The secretary of state sends all official notices, including notices of complaints, to the notary at the address on file with the secretary's office. Requests to obtain copies of or inspect the records in the notary record book are also directed to the notary at the address on file. Failure to change the address may, consequently, result in a revocation of the notary commission if the notary fails to timely respond to a complaint or to a request for public information.

(c) A notary public who removes his or her residence from Texas vacates the office of notary public and must surrender the notary commission to the secretary of state.

§87.60 Electronic Submission

(a) The secretary of state may develop a system for electronic submission of the application for notary public commission, the notary bond, and the statement of officer. On implementation, the secretary of state will authorize the submission of these documents electronically on behalf of a notary under the following terms and conditions:

  (1) the submitter must comply with the technical specifications contained in the *eNotary Web Service Consumer's Guide* available through the Information Technology Division of the Office of the Secretary of State;

  (2) the notary application and the statement of officer signed by the applicant and the surety bond signed by an officer or attorney-in-fact for the surety must be attached to the electronic submission as an image in the format specified in the *eNotary Web Service Consumer's Guide;* and

  (3) all fees must be paid by prepaid account, LegalEase® or credit card.

(b) If the applicant is commissioned, the secretary of state will return the commission and the educational materials to the notary by regular mail. On commission, the applicable fees will be charged to the prepaid account, LegalEase® or the credit card.

(c) If the application is rejected, the secretary of state will return a notice of the rejection to the submitter electronically. On rejection, no fees are charged to the account, LegalEase® or to the credit card.

(d) Status of a notary application may be checked on SOSDirect.

(e) If the submitter is not able to consistently comply with the technical specifications and the submissions are failing as a result, the secretary of state may revoke the privilege of the submitter to submit electronically until all technical issues are resolved to the satisfaction of the secretary of state.

(f) As part of the electronic submission, the submitter is responsible for accurately entering the data elements related to the application. Repeated and consistent entry errors may result in a revocation of the privilege of the submitter to submit electronically.

§87.61 Records Retention for Electronic Submissions

The submitter should retain the original signed application and statement of officer for the duration of the commission to which those documents apply. If the submitter intends to destroy the original documents prior to expiration of the commission, the submitter should confirm with the secretary of state that the image file transmitted with the application is stored and available in the secretary of state's computer system.

§87.62 Applications on Behalf of an Applicant with a Criminal Conviction

The secretary of state will not accept electronic applications on behalf of an applicant who has been convicted of a felony or a crime of moral turpitude. The application under these circumstances (along with the statement of officer, the bond, the explanation of the criminal conviction and the applicable fees) must be delivered to the secretary of state by mail, courier or personal delivery.

§87.70 Qualification by an Escrow Officer Residing in an Adjacent State

(a) An applicant who is qualified as an escrow officer within the meaning assigned by §2652.051, Insurance Code, is not required to be a resident of Texas if the applicant is a resident of New Mexico, Oklahoma, Arkansas or Louisiana.

(b) The secretary of state shall commission the applicant if, notwithstanding the residency requirements, the applicant satisfies the conditions of subsection (a) of this section and §87.3 of this title (relating to Issuance of the Notary Public Commission by the Secretary of State).

(c) A notary public, appointed under this section, who ceases to be qualified under this section, must voluntarily surrender the notary public commission.

Chapter 121 Civil Practice and Remedies Code

Sec. 121.001. OFFICERS WHO MAY TAKE ACKNOWLEDGMENTS OR PROOFS

(a) An acknowledgment or proof of a written instrument may be taken in this state by:

   (1) a clerk of a district court;

   (2) a judge or clerk of a county court;

   (3) a notary public;

   (4) a county tax assessor-collector or an employee of the county tax assessor-collector if the instrument is required or authorized to be filed in the office of the county tax assessor-collector; or

   (5) an employee of a personal bond office if the acknowledgment or proof of a written instrument is

required or authorized by Article 17.04, Code of Criminal Procedure.

(b) An acknowledgment or proof of a written instrument may be taken outside this state, but inside the United States or its territories, by:

(1) a clerk of a court of record having a seal;

(2) a commissioner of deeds appointed under the laws of this state; or

(3) a notary public.

(c) An acknowledgment or proof of a written instrument may be taken outside the United States or its territories by:

(1) a minister, commissioner, or charge d'affaires of the United States who is a resident of and is accredited in the country where the acknowledgment or proof is taken;

(2) a consul-general, consul, vice-consul, commercial agent, vice-commercial agent, deputy consul, or consular agent of the United States who is a resident of the country where the acknowledgment or proof is taken; or

(3) a notary public or any other official authorized to administer oaths in the jurisdiction where the acknowledgment or proof is taken.

(d) A commissioned officer of the United States Armed Forces or of a United States Armed Forces Auxiliary may take an acknowledgment or proof of a written instrument of a member of the armed forces, a member of an armed forces auxiliary, or a member's spouse. If an acknowledgment or a proof is taken under this subsection, it is presumed, absent pleading and proof to the contrary, that the commissioned officer who signed was a commissioned officer on the date that the officer signed, and that the acknowledging person was a member of the authorized group of military personnel or spouses. The failure of the commissioned officer to attach an official seal to the certificate of acknowledgment or proof of an instrument does not invalidate the acknowledgment or proof.

Sec. 121.002. CORPORATE ACKNOWLEDGMENTS

(a) An employee of a corporation is not disqualified because of his employment from taking an acknowledgment or proof of a written instrument in which the corporation has an interest.

(b) An officer who is a shareholder in a corporation is not disqualified from taking an acknowledgment or proof of an instrument in which the corporation has an interest unless:

  (1) the corporation has 1,000 or fewer shareholders; and

  (2) the officer owns more than one-tenth of one percent of the issued and outstanding stock.

Sec. 121.003. AUTHORITY OF OFFICERS

In a proceeding to prove a written instrument, an officer authorized by this chapter to take an acknowledgment or a proof of a written instrument is also authorized to:

(1) administer oaths;

(2) employ and swear interpreters; and

(3) issue subpoenas.

Sec. 121.004. METHOD OF ACKNOWLEDGMENT

(a) To acknowledge a written instrument for recording, the grantor or person who executed the instrument must appear before an officer and must state that he executed the instrument for the purposes and consideration expressed in it.

(b) The officer shall:

  (1) make a certificate of the acknowledgment;

  (2) sign the certificate; and

(3) seal the certificate with the seal of office.

(c) The failure of a notary public to attach an official seal to a certificate of an acknowledgement or proof of a written instrument made outside this state but inside the United States or its territories renders the acknowledgement or proof invalid only if the jurisdiction in which the certificate is made requires the notary public to attach the seal.

(d) The application of an embossed seal is not required on an electronically transmitted certificate of an acknowledgement.

Sec. 121.005. PROOF OF IDENTITY OF ACKNOWLEDGING PERSON

(a) An officer may not take the acknowledgment of a written instrument unless the officer knows or has satisfactory evidence that the acknowledging person is the person who executed the instrument and is described in it. An officer may accept, as satisfactory evidence of the identity of an acknowledging person, only:

(1) the oath of a credible witness personally known to the officer;

(2) a current identification card or other document issued by the federal government or any state government that contains the photograph and signature of the acknowledging person; or

(3) with respect to a deed or other instrument relating to a residential real estate transaction, a current passport issued by a foreign country.

(b) Except in a short form certificate of acknowledgment authorized by Section 121.008, the officer must note in the certificate of acknowledgment that:

(1) he personally knows the acknowledging person; or

(2) evidence of a witness or an identification card or other document was used to identify the acknowledging person.

Sec. 121.006. ALTERATION OF AUTHORIZED FORMS; DEFINITION

(a) An acknowledgment form provided by this chapter may be altered as circumstances require. The authorization of a form does not prevent the use of other forms. The marital status or other status of the acknowledging person may be shown after the person's name.

(b) In an acknowledgment form "acknowledged" means:

(1) in the case of a natural person, that the person personally appeared before the officer taking the acknowledgment and acknowledged executing the instrument for the purposes and consideration expressed in it;

(2) in the case of a person as principal by an attorney-in-fact for the principal, that the attorney-in-fact personally appeared before the officer taking the acknowledgment and that the attorney-in-fact acknowledged executing the instrument as the act of the principal for the purposes and consideration expressed in it;

(3) in the case of a partnership by a partner or partners acting for the partnership, that the partner or partners personally appeared before the officer taking the acknowledgment and acknowledged executing the instrument as the act of the partnership for the purposes and consideration expressed in it;

(4) in the case of a corporation by a corporate officer or agent, that the corporate officer or agent personally appeared before the officer taking the acknowledgment

and that the corporate officer or agent acknowledged executing the instrument in the capacity stated, as the act of the corporation, for the purposes and consideration expressed in it; and

(5) in the case of a person acknowledging as a public officer, trustee, executor or administrator of an estate, guardian, or other representative, that the person personally appeared before the officer taking the acknowledgment and acknowledged executing the instrument by proper authority in the capacity stated and for the purposes and consideration expressed in it.

Sec. 121.007. FORM FOR ORDINARY CERTIFICATE OF ACKNOWLEDGMENT

The form of an ordinary certificate of acknowledgment must be substantially as follows:

"The State of ____________,

"County of ____________,

"Before me ____________ (here insert the name and character of the officer) on this day personally appeared ________________, known to me (or proved to me on the oath of ________________ or through ________________ (description of identity card or other document)) to be the person whose name is subscribed to the foregoing instrument and acknowledged to me that he executed the same for the purposes and consideration therein expressed.

(Seal) "Given under my hand and seal of office this ________ day of ____________, A.D., ________."

Sec. 121.008. SHORT FORMS FOR CERTIFICATES OF ACKNOWLEDGMENT

(a) The forms for certificates of acknowledgment provided by this section may be used as alternatives to other authorized forms. They may be referred to as "statutory forms of acknowledgment."

(b) Short forms for certificates of acknowledgment include:

(1) For a natural person acting in his own right:

State of Texas

County of ____________

This instrument was acknowledged before me on (date) by (name or names of person or persons acknowledging).

(Signature of officer)

(Title of officer)

My commission expires: ________

(2) For a natural person as principal acting by attorney-in-fact:

State of Texas

County of ____________

This instrument was acknowledged before me on (date) by (name of attorney-in-fact) as attorney-in-fact on behalf of (name of principal).

(Signature of officer)

(Title of officer)

My commission expires: ________

(3) For a partnership acting by one or more partners:
State of Texas

County of ____________

This instrument was acknowledged before me on (date) by (name of acknowledging partner or partners), partner(s) on behalf of (name of partnership), a partnership.

(Signature of officer)

(Title of officer)

My commission expires: ________

(4) For a corporation:
State of Texas

County of ____________

This instrument was acknowledged before me on (date) by (name of officer), (title of officer) of (name of corporation acknowledging) a (state of incorporation) corporation, on behalf of said corporation.

(Signature of officer)

(Title of officer)

My commission expires: ________

(5) For a public officer, trustee, executor, administrator, guardian, or other representative:
State of Texas

County of ____________

This instrument was acknowledged before me on (date) by (name of representative) as (title of representative) of (name of entity or person represented).

(Signature of officer)

(Title of officer)

My commission expires: ________

Sec. 121.009. PROOF OF ACKNOWLEDGMENT BY WITNESS

(a) To prove a written instrument for recording, at least one of the witnesses who signed the instrument must personally appear before an officer who is authorized by this chapter to take acknowledgments or proofs and must swear:

  (1) either that he saw the grantor or person who executed the instrument sign it or that that person acknowledged in the presence of the witness that he executed the instrument for the purposes and consideration expressed in it; and

  (2) that he signed the instrument at the request of the grantor or person who executed the instrument.

(b) The officer must make a certificate of the testimony of the witness and must sign and officially seal the certificate.

(c) The officer may take the testimony of a witness only if the officer personally knows or has satisfactory evidence on the oath of a credible witness that the individual testifying is the person who signed the instrument as a witness. If evidence is used to identify the witness who signed the instrument, the officer must note the use of the evidence in the certificate of acknowledgment.

Sec. 121.010. FORM OF CERTIFICATE FOR PROOF BY WITNESS

When the execution of a written instrument is proved by a witness, the certificate of the officer must be substantially as follows:

"The State of ____________,

"County of ____________.

"Before me, ________ (here insert the name and character of the officer), on this day personally appeared ____________, known to me (or proved to me on the oath of ____________), to be the person whose name is subscribed as a witness to the foregoing instrument of writing, and after being duly sworn by me stated on oath that he saw ____________, the grantor or person who executed the foregoing instrument, subscribe the same (or that the grantor or person who executed such instrument of writing acknowledged in his presence that he had executed the same for the purposes and consideration therein expressed), and that he had signed the same as a witness at the request of the grantor (or person who executed the same.)

(Seal) "Given under my hand and seal of office this ______ day of ____________, A.D., ____________."

Sec. 121.011. PROOF OF ACKNOWLEDGMENT BY HANDWRITING

(a) The execution of an instrument may be established for recording by proof of the handwriting of persons who signed the instrument only if:

(1) the grantor of the instrument and all of the witnesses are dead;

(2) the grantor and all of the witnesses are not residents of this state;

(3) the residences of the grantor and the witnesses are unknown to the person seeking to prove the instrument and cannot be ascertained;

(4) the witnesses have become legally incompetent to testify; or

(5) the grantor of the instrument refuses to acknowledge the execution of the instrument and all of the witnesses are dead, not residents of this state, or legally incompetent or their places of residence are unknown.

(b) If the grantor or person who executed the instrument signed his name to the instrument, its execution must be proved by evidence of the handwriting of that person and at least one witness who signed the instrument. If the grantor or person who executed the instrument signed the instrument by making his mark, its execution must be proved by the handwriting of at least two of the witnesses who signed the instrument.

(c) Evidence taken for proof of handwriting must give the residence of the testifying witness. A testifying witness must have known the person whose handwriting is being proved and must be well acquainted with the handwriting in question and recognize it as genuine.

(d) Evidence offered for proof of handwriting must be given in writing by the deposition or affidavit of two or more disinterested persons. The evidence must satisfactorily prove to the officer each of the requirements provided by this section. The officer taking the proof must certify the witnesses' testimony. The officer must sign, officially seal, and attach this certificate to the instrument with the depositions or affidavits of the witnesses.

Sec. 121.012. RECORD OF ACKNOWLEDGMENT

(a) An officer authorized by law to take an acknowledgment or proof of a written instrument required or permitted by law to be recorded must enter in a well-bound book and officially sign a short statement of each acknowledgment or proof. The statement must contain the date that the acknowledgment or proof was taken, the date of the instrument, and the names of the grantor and grantee of the instrument.

(b) If the execution of the instrument is acknowledged by the grantor of the instrument, the statement must also contain:
  (1) the grantor's known or alleged residence;
  (2) whether the grantor is personally known to the officer; and
  (3) if the grantor is unknown to the officer, the name and residence of the person who introduced the grantor to the officer, if any.

(c) If the execution of the instrument is proved by a witness who signed the instrument, the statement must also contain:
  (1) the name of the witness;
  (2) the known or alleged residence of the witness;
  (3) whether the witness is personally known to the officer; and
  (4) if the witness is unknown to the officer, the name and known or alleged residence of the person who introduced the witness to the officer, if any.

(d) If land is charged or conveyed by the instrument, the statement must also contain:
  (1) the name of the original grantee; and
  (2) the name of the county in which the land is located.

(e) The statements of acknowledgment recorded by the officer are original public records, open for public inspection and examination at all reasonable times. The officer must deliver the book to his successor in office.

Sec. 121.013. SUBPOENA OF WITNESS; ATTACHMENT

(a) On the sworn application of a person interested in the proof of an instrument required or permitted by law to be recorded, stating that a witness to the instrument refuses to appear and testify regarding the execution of the instrument and that the instrument cannot be proven without the evidence of the witness, an officer authorized to take proofs of instruments shall issue a subpoena requiring the witness to appear before the officer and testify about the execution of the instrument.

(b) If the witness fails to obey the subpoena, the officer has the same powers to enforce the attendance and compel the answers of the witness as does a district judge. Attachment may not be issued, however, unless the witness receives or is tendered the same compensation that is made to witnesses in other cases. An officer may not require the witness to leave his county of residence, but if the witness is temporarily present in the county where the execution of the instrument is sought to be proven for registration, he may be required to appear.

Sec. 121.014. ACTION FOR DAMAGES

A person injured by the failure, refusal, or neglect of an officer to comply with a provision of this chapter has a cause of action against the officer to recover damages resulting from the failure, refusal, or neglect of the officer.

Sec. 121.015. PRIVATE SEAL OR SCROLL NOT REQUIRED

A private seal or scroll may not be required on a written instrument other than an instrument made by a corporation.

Rule 176 Texas Rules of Civil Procedure (subpoenas)

176.1 Form

Every subpoena must be issued in the name of "The State of Texas" and must:

(a) state the style of the suit and its cause number;
(b) state the court in which the suit is pending;
(c) state the date on which the subpoena is issued;
(d) identify the person to whom the subpoena is directed;
(e) state the time, place, and nature of the action required by the person to whom the subpoena is directed, as provided in Rule 176.2;
(f) identify the party at whose instance the subpoena is issued, and the party's attorney of record, if any;
(g) state the text of Rule 176.8(a); and(h) be signed by the person issuing the subpoena.

176.2 Required Actions

A subpoena must command the person to whom it is directed to do either or both of the following:

(a) attend and give testimony at a deposition, hearing, or trial;
(b) produce and permit inspection and copying of designated documents or tangible things in the possession, custody, or control of that person.

176.3 Limitations

(a) Range. A person may not be required by subpoena to appear or produce documents or other things in a county that is more than 150 miles from where the person resides or is served. However, a person whose appearance or production at a deposition may be compelled by notice alone under Rules 199.3 or 200.2 may be required to appear and produce documents or other things at any location permitted under Rules 199.2(b)(2).
(b) Use for discovery. A subpoena may not be used for discovery to an extent, in a manner, or at a time other than as provided by the rules governing discovery.

176.4 Who May Issue

A subpoena may be issued by:

(a) the clerk of the appropriate district, county, or justice court, who must provide the party requesting the subpoena with an original and a copy for each witness to be completed by the party;
(b) an attorney authorized to practice in the State of Texas, as an officer of the court; or
(c) an officer authorized to take depositions in this State, who must issue the subpoena immediately on a request accompanied by a notice to take a deposition under Rules 199 or 200, or a notice under Rule 205.3, and who may also serve the notice with the subpoena.

176.5 Service.

(a) Manner of service. A subpoena may be served at any place within the State of Texas by any sheriff or constable of the State of Texas, or any person who is not a party and is 18 years of age or older. A subpoena must be served by delivering a copy to the witness and tendering to that person any fees required by law. If the witness is a party and is represented by an attorney of record in the proceeding, the subpoena may be served on the witness's attorney of record.
(b) Proof of service. Proof of service must be made by filing either:
    (1) the witness's signed written memorandum attached to the subpoena showing that the witness accepted the subpoena; or
    (2) a statement by the person who made the service stating the date, time, and manner of service, and the name of the person served.

176.6 Response

(a) Compliance required. Except as provided in this subdivision, a person served with a subpoena must comply with the command stated therein unless discharged by the court or by the party summoning such witness. A person commanded to appear and give testimony must remain at the place of deposition, hearing, or trial from day to day until discharged by the court or by the party summoning the witness.

(b) Organizations. If a subpoena commanding testimony is directed to a corporation, partnership, association, governmental agency, or other organization, and the matters on which examination is requested are described with reasonable particularity, the organization must designate one or more persons to testify on its behalf as to matters known or reasonably available to the organization.

(c) Production of documents or tangible things. A person commanded to produce documents or tangible things need not appear in person at the time and place of production unless the person is also commanded to attend and give testimony, either in the same subpoena or a separate one. A person must produce documents as they are kept in the usual course of business or must organize and label them to correspond with the categories in the demand. A person may withhold material or information claimed to be privileged but must comply with Rule 193.3. A nonparty's production of a document authenticates the document for use against the nonparty to the same extent as a party's production of a document is authenticated for use against the party under Rule 193.7.

(d) Objections. A person commanded to produce and permit inspection or copying of designated documents and things may serve on the party requesting issuance of the subpoena - before the time specified for compliance - written objections to producing any or all of the designated materials. A person need not comply with the part of a subpoena to which objection is made as provided in this paragraph unless ordered to do so by the court. The party requesting the subpoena may move for such an order at any time after an objection is made.

(e) Protective orders. A person commanded to appear at a deposition, hearing, or trial, or to produce and permit inspection and copying of designated documents and things, and any other person affected by the subpoena, may move for a protective order under Rule 192.6(b)--before the time specified for compliance--either in the court in which the action is pending or in a district court in the county where the subpoena was served. The person must serve the motion on all parties in accordance with Rule 21a. A person need not comply with the part of a subpoena from which protection is sought under this paragraph unless ordered to do so by the court. The party requesting the subpoena may seek such an order at any time after the motion for protection is filed.

(f) Trial subpoenas. A person commanded to attend and give testimony, or to produce documents or things, at a hearing or trial, may object or move for protective order before the court at the time and place specified for compliance, rather than under paragraphs (d) and (e).

176.7 Protection of Person from Undue Burden and Expense

A party causing a subpoena to issue must take reasonable steps to avoid imposing undue burden or expense on the person served. In ruling on objections or motions for protection, the court must provide a person served with a subpoena an adequate time for compliance, protection from disclosure of privileged material or information, and protection from undue burden or expense. The court may impose reasonable conditions on compliance with a subpoena, including compensating the witness for undue hardship.

176.8 Enforcement of Subpoena

(a) Contempt. Failure by any person without adequate excuse to obey a subpoena served upon that person may be deemed a contempt of the court from which the subpoena is issued or a district court in the county in which the subpoena is served, and may be punished by fine or confinement, or both.

(b) Proof of payment of fees required for fine or attachment. A fine may not be imposed, nor a person served with a subpoena attached, for failure to comply with a subpoena without proof by affidavit of the party requesting the subpoena or the party's attorney of record that all fees due the witness by law were paid or tendered.

Chapter 602 Texas Government Code (Administration of Oaths)

Sec. 602.002. OATH MADE IN TEXAS

An oath made in this state may be administered and a certificate of the fact given by:

(1) a judge, retired judge, or clerk of a municipal court;
(2) a judge, retired judge, senior judge, clerk, or commissioner of a court of record;
(3) a justice of the peace or a clerk of a justice court;
(4) an associate judge, magistrate, master, referee, or criminal law hearing officer;
(5) a notary public;
(6) a member of a board or commission created by a law of this state, in a matter pertaining to a duty of the board or commission;

(7) a person employed by the Texas Ethics Commission who has a duty related to a report required by Title 15, Election Code, in a matter pertaining to that duty;
(8) a county tax assessor-collector or an employee of the county tax assessor-collector if the oath relates to a document that is required or authorized to be filed in the office of the county tax assessor-collector;
(9) the secretary of state or a former secretary of state;
(10)an employee of a personal bond office, or an employee of a county, who is employed to obtain information required to be obtained under oath if the oath is required or authorized by Article 17.04 or by Article 26.04(n) or (o), Code of Criminal Procedure;
(11)the lieutenant governor or a former lieutenant governor;
(12)the speaker of the house of representatives or a former speaker of the house of representatives;
(13)the governor or a former governor;
(14)a legislator or retired legislator;
(15)the attorney general or a former attorney general;
(16)the secretary or clerk of a municipality in a matter pertaining to the official business of the municipality; or
(17)a peace officer described by Article 2.12, Code of Criminal Procedure, if:
(18)the oath is administered when the officer is engaged in the performance of the officer's duties; and
(19)the administration of the oath relates to the officer's duties.

Sec. 602.003. OATH MADE OUTSIDE TEXAS BUT INSIDE UNITED STATES

An oath made outside this state but inside the United States or its territories may be administered and a certificate of the fact given by:

(1) a clerk of a court of record having a seal;
(2) a commissioner of deeds appointed under a law of this state; or

(3) a notary public.

Sec. 602.004. OATH MADE OUTSIDE UNITED STATES

An oath made outside the United States and its territories may be administered and a certificate of the fact given by:

(1) a minister, commissioner, or charge d'affaires of the United States who resides in and is accredited to the country where the oath or affidavit is made;
(2) a consul-general, consul, vice-consul, commercial agent, vice-commercial agent, deputy consul, or consular agent of the United States who resides in the country where the oath or affidavit is made; or
(3) a notary public.

Sec. 602.005. OATH MADE BY MEMBER OF ARMED FORCES OR BY MEMBER'S SPOUSE

(a) A commissioned officer of the United States armed forces or of a United States armed forces auxiliary may administer an oath made by a member of the armed forces, a member of an armed forces auxiliary, or a member's spouse and may give a certificate of the fact.
(b) Unless there is pleading or evidence to the contrary, a certificate signed under this section that is offered in evidence establishes that:
    (1) the commissioned officer who signed was a commissioned officer on the date the officer signed; and
    (2) the person who made the oath or affidavit was a member of the armed forces or an armed forces auxiliary or was a member's spouse when the oath was made.

(c) An oath is not invalid because the commissioned officer who certified the oath did not attach an official seal to the certificate.

Sec. 602.006. OATH OF OFFICE

An oath of office may be administered and a certificate of the fact given by a member of the legislature.

Chapter 603 Texas Government Code (Provision of Documents and Fees of Office)

Sec. 603.001. DEFINITION

In this chapter, "document" includes any instrument, paper, or other record.

Sec. 603.002. COPIES OF DOCUMENTS AVAILABLE TO PUBLIC

The secretary of state, Commissioner of the General Land Office, comptroller, commissioner of agriculture, Banking Commissioner, state librarian, or attorney general:

(1) shall furnish to a person on request a certified copy, under seal, of any document in the officer's office that is available under law to that person; and
(2) may not demand or collect a fee from an officer of the state for a copy of any document in the respective offices or for a certificate in relation to a matter in the respective offices if the copy is required in the performance of an official duty of the office of the state officer requesting the copy.

Sec. 603.003. COPIES FOR CLAIMS RELATING TO MILITARY SERVICE

(a) A county clerk, district clerk, or other public official on request shall furnish without cost to a person or the person's guardian, dependent, or heir one or more certified copies of a document that is in the custody of or on file in the county clerk's, district clerk's, or other public official's office if:

(1) the person or the person's guardian, dependent, or heir is eligible to make a claim against the United States government because of service in the United States armed forces or an auxiliary service, including the maritime service or the merchant marine; and

(2) the document is necessary to prove the claim.

(b) The issuance of a certified copy under this section may not be considered in determining the maximum fee of the office.

Sec. 603.004. FEES FOR CERTIFICATES OR COPIES OF DOCUMENTS

(a) Except as otherwise provided by law, the secretary of state, land commissioner, comptroller, commissioner of agriculture, Banking Commissioner, state librarian, attorney general, or other officer of the state or a head of a state department shall collect the following fees for the following services:

(1) a copy, other than a photographic copy, of a document in an office in English, for each page or fraction of a page, $1.50;

(2) a copy, other than a photographic copy, of a document in an office in a language other than English, for each page or fraction of a page, $2;

(3) a translated copy of a document in an office, the greater of $.03 for each word or $5;

(4) a copy of a plat or map in an office, a fee the officer of the office in which the copy is made may establish with reference to the amount of labor, supplies, and materials required; or

(5) a sealed certificate affixed to a copy, including a certificate affixed to a photographic copy, $1.

(b) The state librarian may charge for a photographic copy a fee determined by the Texas State Library and Archives Commission with reference to the amount of labor, supplies, and materials required.

Sec. 603.005. FEE FOR ACKNOWLEDGMENT

An officer who is authorized by law to take acknowledgment or proof of a deed or other written instrument shall receive the same fee a notary public may receive for the same service.

Sec. 603.006. FEE BOOK

An officer who by law may charge a fee for a service shall keep a fee book and shall enter in the book all fees charged for services rendered.

Sec. 603.007. BILL FOR FEES

A fee under this chapter is not payable to a person until a clerk or officer produces, or is ready to produce, a bill in writing containing the details of the fee to the person who owes the fee. The bill must be signed by the clerk or officer to whom the fee is due or who charges the fee or by the successor in office or legal representative of the clerk or officer.

Sec. 603.008. POSTING OF FEES REQUIRED

A county judge, clerk of a district or county court, sheriff, justice of the peace, constable, or notary public shall keep posted at all times in a conspicuous place in the respective offices a complete list of fees the person may charge by law.

Sec. 603.009. DISPOSITION OF FEES

(a) Except as provided by this section, an officer required to collect a fee under Section 603.004 shall deposit the fee in the state treasury to the credit of the general revenue fund.

(b) Repealed by Acts 1999, 76th Leg., ch. 62, Sec. 7.61, eff. Sept. 1, 1999.

(c) The Texas Employment Commission shall deposit fees in accordance with federal law.

(d) The Texas State Library and Archives Commission shall retain fees collected under this chapter by the state librarian.

Sec. 603.010. OVERCHARGING OF FEES; PENALTY

An officer named in this chapter who demands and receives a higher fee than authorized under this chapter or a fee that is not authorized under this chapter is liable to the aggrieved person for four times the amount unlawfully demanded and received.

Chapter 552 Texas Government Code (Public Information)

Sec. 552.001. POLICY; CONSTRUCTION

(a) Under the fundamental philosophy of the American constitutional form of representative government that adheres to the principle that government is the servant and not the master of the people, it is the policy of this state that each person is entitled, unless otherwise expressly provided by law, at all times to complete information about the affairs of government and the official acts of public officials and employees. The people, in delegating authority, do not give their public servants the right to decide what is good for the people to know and what is not good for them to know. The people insist on remaining informed so that they may retain control over the instruments they have created. The provisions of this chapter shall be liberally construed to implement this policy.

(b) This chapter shall be liberally construed in favor of granting a request for information.

Sec. 552.147. SOCIAL SECURITY NUMBERS

(a) Except as provided by Subsection (a-1), the social security number of a living person is excepted from the requirements of Section 552.021, but is not confidential under this section and this section does not make the social security number of a living person confidential under another provision of this chapter or other law.

  (1) The social security number of an employee of a school district in the custody of the district is confidential.

(b) A governmental body may redact the social security number of a living person from any information the governmental body discloses under Section 552.021 without the necessity of requesting a decision from the attorney general under Subchapter G.

(c) Notwithstanding any other law, a county or district clerk may disclose in the ordinary course of business a social security number that is contained in information held by the clerk's office, and that disclosure is not official misconduct and does not subject the clerk to civil or criminal liability of any kind under the law of this state, including any claim for damages in a lawsuit or the criminal penalty imposed by Section 552.352.

(d) Unless another law requires a social security number to be maintained in a government document, on written request from an individual or the individual's representative the clerk shall redact within a reasonable amount of time all but the last four digits of the individual's social security number from information maintained in the clerk's official public records, including electronically stored information maintained by or under the control of the clerk. The individual or the individual's representative must identify, using a form provided by the clerk, the specific document or documents from which the partial social security number shall be redacted.

Sec. 552.351. DESTRUCTION, REMOVAL, OR ALTERATION OF PUBLIC INFORMATION

(a) A person commits an offense if the person wilfully destroys, mutilates, removes without permission as provided by this chapter, or alters public information.

(b) An offense under this section is a misdemeanor punishable by:

 (1) a fine of not less than $25 or more than $4,000;

 (2) confinement in the county jail for not less than three days or more than three months; or

 (3) both the fine and confinement.

(c) It is an exception to the application of Subsection (a) that the public information was transferred under Section 441.204.

Sec. 552.352. DISTRIBUTION OR MISUSE OF CONFIDENTIAL INFORMATION

(a) A person commits an offense if the person distributes information considered confidential under the terms of this chapter.

(a-1) An officer or employee of a governmental body who obtains access to confidential information under Section 552.008 commits an offense if the officer or employee knowingly:

(1) uses the confidential information for a purpose other than the purpose for which the information was received or for a purpose unrelated to the law that permitted the officer or employee to obtain access to the information, including solicitation of political contributions or solicitation of clients;

(2) permits inspection of the confidential information by a person who is not authorized to inspect the information; or

(3) discloses the confidential information to a person who is not authorized to receive the information.

(a-2) For purposes of Subsection (a-1), a member of an advisory committee to a governmental body who obtains access to confidential information in that capacity is considered to be an officer or employee of the governmental body.

(b) An offense under this section is a misdemeanor punishable by:

(1) a fine of not more than $1,000;

(2) confinement in the county jail for not more than six months; or

(3) both the fine and confinement.

(c) A violation under this section constitutes official misconduct.

Sec. 552.353. FAILURE OR REFUSAL OF OFFICER FOR PUBLIC INFORMATION TO PROVIDE ACCESS TO OR COPYING OF PUBLIC INFORMATION

(a) An officer for public information, or the officer's agent, commits an offense if, with criminal negligence, the officer or the officer's agent fails or refuses to give access to, or to permit or provide copying of, public information to a requestor as provided by this chapter.

(b) It is an affirmative defense to prosecution under Subsection (a) that the officer for public information reasonably believed that public access to the requested information was not required and that:

- (1) the officer acted in reasonable reliance on a court order or a written interpretation of this chapter contained in an opinion of a court of record or of the attorney general issued under Subchapter G;
- (2) the officer requested a decision from the attorney general in accordance with Subchapter G, and the decision is pending; or
- (3) not later than the 10th calendar day after the date of receipt of a decision by the attorney general that the information is public, the officer or the governmental body for whom the defendant is the officer for public information filed a petition for a declaratory judgment against the attorney general in a Travis County district court seeking relief from compliance with the decision of the attorney general, as provided by Section 552.324, and the cause is pending.

(c) It is an affirmative defense to prosecution under Subsection (a) that a person or entity has, not later than the 10th calendar day after the date of receipt by a governmental body of a decision by the attorney general that the information is public, filed a cause of action seeking relief from compliance with the decision of the attorney general, as provided by Section 552.325, and the cause is pending.

(d) It is an affirmative defense to prosecution under Subsection (a) that the defendant is the agent of an officer for public information and that the agent reasonably relied on the written instruction of the officer for public information not to disclose the public information requested.

(e) An offense under this section is a misdemeanor punishable by:

 (1) a fine of not more than $1,000;

 (2) confinement in the county jail for not more than six months; or

 (3) both the fine and confinement.

(f) A violation under this section constitutes official misconduct.

Title 8 Texas Penal Code

Sec. 36.01. DEFINITIONS

In this chapter:

(1) "Custody" means:

 (A) detained or under arrest by a peace officer; or

 (B) under restraint by a public servant pursuant to an order of a court.

(2) "Party official" means a person who holds any position or office in a political party, whether by election, appointment, or employment.

(3) "Benefit" means anything reasonably regarded as pecuniary gain or pecuniary advantage, including benefit to any other person in whose welfare the beneficiary has a direct and substantial interest.

(4) "Vote" means to cast a ballot in an election regulated by law.

Sec. 36.02. BRIBERY

(a) A person commits an offense if he intentionally or knowingly offers, confers, or agrees to confer on another, or solicits, accepts, or agrees to accept from another:

(1) any benefit as consideration for the recipient's decision, opinion, recommendation, vote, or other exercise of discretion as a public servant, party official, or voter;

(2) any benefit as consideration for the recipient's decision, vote, recommendation, or other exercise of official discretion in a judicial or administrative proceeding;

(3) any benefit as consideration for a violation of a duty imposed by law on a public servant or party official; or

(4) any benefit that is a political contribution as defined by Title 15, Election Code, or that is an expenditure made and reported in accordance with Chapter 305, Government Code, if the benefit was offered, conferred, solicited, accepted, or agreed to pursuant to an express agreement to take or withhold a specific exercise of official discretion if such exercise of official discretion would not have been taken or withheld but for the benefit; notwithstanding any rule of evidence or jury instruction allowing factual inferences in the absence of certain evidence, direct evidence of the express agreement shall be required in any prosecution under this subdivision.

(b) It is no defense to prosecution under this section that a person whom the actor sought to influence was not qualified to act in the desired way whether because he had not yet assumed office or he lacked jurisdiction or for any other reason.

(c) It is no defense to prosecution under this section that the benefit is not offered or conferred or that the benefit is not solicited or accepted until after:

(1) the decision, opinion, recommendation, vote, or other exercise of discretion has occurred; or

(2) the public servant ceases to be a public servant.

(d) It is an exception to the application of Subdivisions (1), (2), and (3) of Subsection (a) that the benefit is a political contribution as defined by Title 15, Election Code, or an expenditure made and reported in accordance with Chapter 305, Government Code.
(e) An offense under this section is a felony of the second degree.

Sec. 36.03. COERCION OF PUBLIC SERVANT OR VOTER

(a) A person commits an offense if by means of coercion he:
  (1) influences or attempts to influence a public servant in a specific exercise of his official power or a specific performance of his official duty or influences or attempts to influence a public servant to violate the public servant's known legal duty; or
  (2) influences or attempts to influence a voter not to vote or to vote in a particular manner.
(b) An offense under this section is a Class A misdemeanor unless the coercion is a threat to commit a felony, in which event it is a felony of the third degree.
(c) It is an exception to the application of Subsection (a)(1) of this section that the person who influences or attempts to influence the public servant is a member of the governing body of a governmental entity, and that the action that influences or attempts to influence the public servant is an official action taken by the member of the governing body. For the purposes of this subsection, the term "official action" includes deliberations by the governing body of a governmental entity.

Sec. 36.06. OBSTRUCTION OR RETALIATION

(a) A person commits an offense if he intentionally or knowingly harms or threatens to harm another by an unlawful act:
  (1) in retaliation for or on account of the service or status of another as a:

(A) public servant, witness, prospective witness, or informant; or

(B) person who has reported or who the actor knows intends to report the occurrence of a crime; or

(2) to prevent or delay the service of another as a:

(A) public servant, witness, prospective witness, or informant; or

(B) person who has reported or who the actor knows intends to report the occurrence of a crime.

(b) In this section:

(1) "Honorably retired peace officer" means a peace officer who:

(A) did not retire in lieu of any disciplinary action;

(B) was eligible to retire from a law enforcement agency or was ineligible to retire only as a result of an injury received in the course of the officer's employment with the agency; and

(C) is entitled to receive a pension or annuity for service as a law enforcement officer or is not entitled to receive a pension or annuity only because the law enforcement agency that employed the officer does not offer a pension or annuity to its employees.

(2) "Informant" means a person who has communicated information to the government in connection with any governmental function.

(3) "Public servant" includes an honorably retired peace officer.

(c) An offense under this section is a felony of the third degree unless the victim of the offense was harmed or threatened because of the victim's service or status as a juror, in which event the offense is a felony of the second degree.

Sec. 37.01. DEFINITIONS

In this chapter:

(1) "Court record" means a decree, judgment, order, subpoena, warrant, minutes, or other document issued by a court of:
   (A) this state;
   (B) another state;
   (C) the United States;
   (D) a foreign country recognized by an act of congress or a treaty or other international convention to which the United States is a party;
   (E) an Indian tribe recognized by the United States; or
   (F) any other jurisdiction, territory, or protectorate entitled to full faith and credit in this state under the United States Constitution.

(2) "Governmental record" means:
   (A) anything belonging to, received by, or kept by government for information, including a court record;
   (B) anything required by law to be kept by others for information of government;
   (C) a license, certificate, permit, seal, title, letter of patent, or similar document issued by government, by another state, or by the United States;
   (D) a standard proof of motor vehicle liability insurance form described by Section 601.081, Transportation Code, a certificate of an insurance company described by Section 601.083 of that code, a document purporting to be such a form or certificate that is not issued by an insurer authorized to write motor vehicle liability insurance in this state, an electronic submission in a form described by Section 502.046(i), Transportation Code, or an evidence of financial responsibility described by Section 601.053 of that code;

(E) an official ballot or other election record; or

(F) the written documentation a mobile food unit is required to obtain under Section 437.0074, Health and Safety Code.

(3) "Statement" means any representation of fact.

Sec. 37.02. PERJURY

(a) A person commits an offense if, with intent to deceive and with knowledge of the statement's meaning:

(1) he makes a false statement under oath or swears to the truth of a false statement previously made and the statement is required or authorized by law to be made under oath; or

(2) he makes a false unsworn declaration under Chapter 132, Civil Practice and Remedies Code.

(b) An offense under this section is a Class A misdemeanor.

Sec. 37.03. AGGRAVATED PERJURY

(a) A person commits an offense if he commits perjury as defined in Section 37.02, and the false statement:

(1) is made during or in connection with an official proceeding; and

(2) is material.

(b) An offense under this section is a felony of the third degree.

Sec. 37.10. TAMPERING WITH GOVERNMENTAL RECORD

(a) A person commits an offense if he:

(1) knowingly makes a false entry in, or false alteration of, a governmental record;

(2) makes, presents, or uses any record, document, or thing with knowledge of its falsity and with intent that it be taken as a genuine governmental record;
(3) intentionally destroys, conceals, removes, or otherwise impairs the verity, legibility, or availability of a governmental record;
(4) possesses, sells, or offers to sell a governmental record or a blank governmental record form with intent that it be used unlawfully;
(5) makes, presents, or uses a governmental record with knowledge of its falsity; or
(6) possesses, sells, or offers to sell a governmental record or a blank governmental record form with knowledge that it was obtained unlawfully.

(b) It is an exception to the application of Subsection (a)(3) that the governmental record is destroyed pursuant to legal authorization or transferred under Section 441.204, Government Code. With regard to the destruction of a local government record, legal authorization includes compliance with the provisions of Subtitle C, Title 6, Local Government Code.

(c) (c)

(1) Except as provided by Subdivisions (2), (3), and (4) and by Subsection (d), an offense under this section is a Class A misdemeanor unless the actor's intent is to defraud or harm another, in which event the offense is a state jail felony.

Sec. 37.11. IMPERSONATING PUBLIC SERVANT

(a) A person commits an offense if he:

(1) impersonates a public servant with intent to induce another to submit to his pretended official authority or to rely on his pretended official acts; or

(2) knowingly purports to exercise any function of a public servant or of a public office, including that of a judge and court, and the position or office through which he purports to exercise a function of a public servant or public office has no lawful existence under the constitution or laws of this state or of the United States.

(b) An offense under this section is a felony of the third degree.

Sec. 39.01. DEFINITIONS

In this chapter:

(1) "Law relating to a public servant's office or employment" means a law that specifically applies to a person acting in the capacity of a public servant and that directly or indirectly:

(A) imposes a duty on the public servant; or

(B) governs the conduct of the public servant.

(2) "Misuse" means to deal with property contrary to:

(A) an agreement under which the public servant holds the property;

(B) a contract of employment or oath of office of a public servant;

(C) a law, including provisions of the General Appropriations Act specifically relating to government property, that prescribes the manner of custody or disposition of the property; or

(D) a limited purpose for which the property is delivered or received.

Sec. 39.015. CONCURRENT JURISDICTION TO PROSECUTE OFFENSES UNDER THIS CHAPTER

With the consent of the appropriate local county or district attorney, the attorney general has concurrent jurisdiction with that consenting local prosecutor to prosecute an offense under this chapter.

Sec. 39.02. ABUSE OF OFFICIAL CAPACITY

(a) A public servant commits an offense if, with intent to obtain a benefit or with intent to harm or defraud another, he intentionally or knowingly:
   (1) violates a law relating to the public servant's office or employment; or
   (2) misuses government property, services, personnel, or any other thing of value belonging to the government that has come into the public servant's custody or possession by virtue of the public servant's office or employment.

(b) An offense under Subsection (a)(1) is a Class A misdemeanor.

(c) An offense under Subsection (a)(2) is:
   (1) a Class C misdemeanor if the value of the use of the thing misused is less than $20;
   (2) a Class B misdemeanor if the value of the use of the thing misused is $20 or more but less than $500;
   (3) a Class A misdemeanor if the value of the use of the thing misused is $500 or more but less than $1,500;
   (4) a state jail felony if the value of the use of the thing misused is $1,500 or more but less than $20,000;
   (5) a felony of the third degree if the value of the use of the thing misused is $20,000 or more but less than $100,000;
   (6) a felony of the second degree if the value of the use of the thing misused is $100,000 or more but less than $200,000; or

(7) a felony of the first degree if the value of the use of the thing misused is $200,000 or more.

(d) A discount or award given for travel, such as frequent flyer miles, rental car or hotel discounts, or food coupons, are not things of value belonging to the government for purposes of this section due to the administrative difficulty and cost involved in recapturing the discount or award for a governmental entity.

(e) If separate transactions that violate Subsection (a)(2) are conducted pursuant to one scheme or continuing course of conduct, the conduct may be considered as one offense and the value of the use of the things misused in the transactions may be aggregated in determining the classification of the offense.

(f) The value of the use of a thing of value misused under Subsection (a)(2) may not exceed:

(1) the fair market value of the thing at the time of the offense; or

(2) if the fair market value of the thing cannot be ascertained, the cost of replacing the thing within a reasonable time after the offense.

Sec. 39.03. OFFICIAL OPPRESSION

(a) A public servant acting under color of his office or employment commits an offense if he:

(1) intentionally subjects another to mistreatment or to arrest, detention, search, seizure, dispossession, assessment, or lien that he knows is unlawful;

(2) intentionally denies or impedes another in the exercise or enjoyment of any right, privilege, power, or immunity, knowing his conduct is unlawful; or

(3) intentionally subjects another to sexual harassment.

(b) For purposes of this section, a public servant acts under color of his office or employment if he acts or purports to act in an official capacity or takes advantage of such actual or purported capacity.

(c) In this section, "sexual harassment" means unwelcome sexual advances, requests for sexual favors, or other verbal or physical conduct of a sexual nature, submission to which is made a term or condition of a person's exercise or enjoyment of any right, privilege, power, or immunity, either explicitly or implicitly.

(d) An offense under this section is a Class A misdemeanor, except that an offense is a felony of the third degree if the public servant acted with the intent to impair the accuracy of data reported to the Texas Education Agency through the Public Education Information Management System (PEIMS) described by Section 42.006, Education Code, under a law requiring that reporting.

Sec. 39.06. MISUSE OF OFFICIAL INFORMATION

(a) A public servant commits an offense if, in reliance on information to which he has access by virtue of his office or employment and that has not been made public, he:

  (1) acquires or aids another to acquire a pecuniary interest in any property, transaction, or enterprise that may be affected by the information;

  (2) speculates or aids another to speculate on the basis of the information; or

  (3) as a public servant, including as a principal of a school, coerces another into suppressing or failing to report that information to a law enforcement agency.

(b) A public servant commits an offense if with intent to obtain a benefit or with intent to harm or defraud another, he discloses or uses information for a nongovernmental purpose that:

  (1) he has access to by means of his office or employment; and

  (2) has not been made public.

(c) A person commits an offense if, with intent to obtain a benefit or with intent to harm or defraud another, he solicits or receives from a public servant information that:
   (1) the public servant has access to by means of his office or employment; and
   (2) has not been made public.

(d) In this section, "information that has not been made public" means any information to which the public does not generally have access, and that is prohibited from disclosure under Chapter 552, Government Code.

(e) Except as provided by Subsection (f), an offense under this section is a felony of the third degree.

(f) An offense under Subsection (a)(3) is a Class C misdemeanor.

Chapter 21

Reference and Example Documents

Disability/Impairment Accommodation Forms

Deaf/Hearing Impaired Written Communication

Written Communication Form

Date:
Title of Document:
Signer Name:

1) May I see your government issued identification?
2) If not already signed, please sign the document.
3) I will point to one of the following questions. Please circle your answer to that question. Please ignore the other question as it does not pertain to your document.
    a. Do you acknowledge that this is your signature and that you signed the document willingly for the purposes stated therein? YES NO
    b. Do you swear (or affirm) under penalties of perjury that the information contained in this document is the truth and that you are signing willingly for the purposes stated therein, so help you God? YES NO

4) When prompted please sign the notary journal and provide a right thumbprint.
5) The fee for today's service is $_________
6) Thank you for your business.

Additional questions or instructions:

Notary Certificate for Signature by Mark (Acknowledgment)

Date:

Title of Document:

____

Signer's Name

____

Signer's Mark

____

Witness Name

____

____

Witness Address

State of Texas

County of ____________________

This instrument was acknowledged before me and this witness on this ________ day of ___________________, 20_____.

____

(Seal) Notary Public, State of Texas

Notary Certificate for Signature by Mark (Jurat)

Date:

Title of Document:

____

Signer's Name

____

Signer's Mark

____

Witness Name

____

____

Witness Address

State of Texas

County of ______________________

Sworn to and subscribed before me and this witness on this _________ day of _____________________, 20______.

____

(Seal) Notary Public, State of Texas

English/Spanish Translations

These translations were taken from Google Translate at http://translate.google.com.

Do you acknowledge that this is your signature and that you signed this document willingly for the purposes stated within?

¿Reconoce usted que esta es su firma y que firmó este documento voluntariamente para los fines declarados dentro?

Please raise your right hand. Do you swear (or affirm) that the information contained in this document is the truth and that you signed this document willingly for the purposes stated within, so help you God?

Por favor, levanten la mano derecha. ¿Jura (o afirmo) que la información contenida en este documento es la verdad y que firmó este documento voluntariamente a los efectos prevenidos en el interior, por lo que ayudará a Dios?

I am sorry, but the law states that I must be able to communicate with you directly. Because we cannot communicate directly, I cannot help you with this document. Please visit with a bilingual attorney or notary public. You will not be charged for your visit with me today.

Lo siento, pero la ley establece que yo debo ser capaz de comunicarse con usted directamente. Porque no podemos comunicar directamente, yo no te puedo ayudar con este documento. Visite por favor con un abogado bilingüe o notary public. No se le cobrará por su visita hoy conmigo.

Sample Notary Checklist

Use this checklist after every notarial act to double check your work.

1) Journal entry has been made
2) Identification is valid
3) There are no blank spaces in the document
4) The document has been signed
5) The venue is on the notarial certificate and is correct.
6) The notarial certificate is complete, with proper date
7) Notarial certificate is signed

If all 7 items have been checked and are correct affix your stamp/seal to the document.

Works Cited

Attorney General of Texas. (2005, January 25). *Texas Attorney General Opinion No. GA-0299*. Retrieved May 17, 2014, from Texas Attorney General: https://www.texasattorneygeneral.gov/opinions/opinions/50abbott/op/2005/htm/ga0299.htm

Attorney General of Texas. (2009, June 17). *Texas Attorney General Opinion No. GA-0723*. Retrieved May 17, 2014, from Attorney General of Texas: https://www.oag.state.tx.us/opinions/opinions/50abbott/op/2009/htm/ga-0723.htm

Dictionary.com. (2014, May 17). *Subpoena*. Retrieved May 17, 2014, from Dictionary.com Unabridged: http://dictionary.reference.com/browse/subpoena

Federal Bureau of Investigation. (n.d.). *FBI--Federal Statutes*. Retrieved May 17, 2014, from Federal Bureau of Investigation: http://www.fbi.gov/about-us/investigate/civilrights/federal-statutes

Texas Secretary of State. (2014). *Notary Public Educational Information*. Retrieved May 17, 2014, from Texas Secretary of State: http://www.sos.state.tx.us/statdoc/edinfo.shtml

Texas Supreme Court. (2014, January 23). *Texas Rules of Civil Procedure, Part 2*. Retrieved May 17, 2014, from Texas Supreme Court: http://www.supreme.courts.state.tx.us/rules/trcp/trcp_part_2.pdf

Index

Questions and Comments

If you have a question about proper notary procedures or situations; or if you have a comment or suggestion for a future edition of this book please email me at: notaryfaq@lubbocknotary.com.

With your approval, your question or suggestion may be printed in the next edition; or, if you prefer, your identity will remain anonymous.

www.ingramcontent.com/pod-product-compliance
Lightning Source LLC
Chambersburg PA
CBHW051646170526
45167CB00001B/349

* 9 7 8 1 4 9 9 3 8 6 5 2 3 *